THE METAPHYSICS OF MIND

THE METAPHYSICS OF MIND

ANTHONY KENNY

CLARENDON PRESS · OXFORD
1989

Oxford University Press, Walton Street, Oxford OX2 6DP

Oxford New York Toronto
Delhi Bombay Calcutta Madras Karachi
Petaling Jaya Singapore Hong Kong Tokyo
Nairobi Dar es Salaam Cape Town
Melbourne Auckland
and associated companies in
Berlin Ibadan

Oxford is a trade mark of Oxford University Press

Published in the United States
by Oxford University Press, New York

British Library Cataloguing in Publication Data
Kenny, Anthony 1931–
The metaphysics of mind.
1. Mind. Philosophical perspectives
I. Title
128.2
ISBN 0–19–824965–9

Library of Congress Cataloging in Publication Data
Data available

Typeset by Pentacor Ltd,
High Wycombe, Bucks
Printed in Great Britain by
Biddles Ltd, Guildford & King's Lynn

Preface

FORTY years ago, in 1949, Gilbert Ryle, the Waynflete Professor of Metaphysical Philosophy in the University of Oxford, published a book entitled *The Concept of Mind* (Hutchinson, London). It was, for many years, highly influential, not only among professional philosophers but also among psychologists, linguists, and practitioners of many other disciplines whose concerns overlapped with those of the philosophical profession. Its influence and its reputation derived not only from its intrinsic philosophical interest, but also from its author's unusual gift for presenting technical philosophical arguments in a style of pugnacious lucidity which arrested the attention of the general public.

I count myself among those who owe a great debt to *The Concept of Mind*. When it was published I was an undergraduate student of philosophy at the Gregorian University in Rome. The book was drawn to my attention by Dr (now Bishop) Alan Clark, then *Ripetitore* in philosophy at the Venerable English College in Rome. I found its style exhilaratingly different from that of the scholastic textbooks which were prescribed in the courses of my Pontifical University; yet I came gradually to realize that the philosophical content of the book bore some surprising resemblances to the doctrines of Aristotle and Aquinas who were in theory the standard bearers of the philosophy in which my Jesuit mentors were striving to instruct me.

When, in 1957, I became a graduate student in Oxford I was fortunate both to be able to see *The Concept of Mind* in its local and historical context, and, along with many other novice philosophers, to experience the generosity of its author as teacher and later as colleague. I came to realize that the ideas which were expressed with crudity as well as vivacity by Ryle had been developed more painfully and more subtly by the much greater genius of Wittgenstein. But comparing what I knew at first hand of Ryle with what I heard from others of Wittgenstein, I also came to believe that the lesser talent had been accompanied with a greater humility.

In recent decades, the influence of both Ryle and Wittgenstein seems to have diminished among professional philosophers. In some of his work, Ryle espoused an exaggerated behaviourism which deserved to pass into oblivion. But other insights which the two philosophers shared are no longer in the forefront of philosophical discussion, not because they have been shown to be flawed or inadequate, but simply because of the impact on philosophical fashion of variations in the prestige of a number of non-philosophical disciplines. In the year when *The Concept of Mind* achieves its fortieth anniversary, I have tried in this book to restate some of these insights in gratitude for the friendship of Ryle and in tribute to the genius of Wittgenstein.

It is now twenty-five years since I completed my own first contribution to the philosophy of mind, *Action, Emotion and Will* (Routledge, London, 1963), which was a revision of my Oxford doctoral thesis, 'The Intentionality of Psychological Verbs'. I returned to some of the theses of that book, and attempted to apply them to the treatment of the traditional topic of the freedom of the will in *Will, Freedom and Power* (Blackwell, Oxford, 1975). For many years I have had in mind to write a third book, *Power, Control and Action*, to complete a trilogy of works in the philosophy of action. I have never, in fact, carried out this project. Instead, I have written a number of lectures and papers relating philosophical theses in philosophy of action to their practical applications in ethics, law, and politics (*Freewill and Responsibility*, Routledge, London, 1978; *The Ivory Tower*, Blackwell, Oxford, 1985). I have also written a number of historical studies (*Descartes*, Random House, New York, 1968; *Wittgenstein*, Penguin, Harmondsworth, 1973; *Aquinas*, OUP, Oxford, 1980; *The Legacy of Wittgenstein*, Blackwell, Oxford, 1984) in which I have tried not only to expound the ideas of these philosophers but also to extract from the critical discussion of their work permanently valuable insights into the philosophy of mind.

This book gives me an opportunity not only to pay tribute to the philosophers whose work in the philosophy of mind I most admire, but also to bring together into a comparatively systematic whole my own work in the philosophy of mind scattered through various contexts over twenty-five years.

The structure of this book is modelled on that of *The Concept of*

Mind, and the ten chapters of which it consists divide the field of discussion in almost exactly the same way as the ten chapters which Ryle published in 1949.

My first chapter, like Ryle's, is entitled 'Descartes' Myth'. Like Ryle, I regard the inheritance of Descartes as being the single most substantial obstacle to a correct philosophical understanding of the nature of the human mind. It might have been thought that the polemic of Ryle, and even more the patient conceptual therapy of Wittgenstein, would have exorcized for ever from the writings of philosophers the Cartesian ghost in the machine. But there has been in recent decades an astonishing florescence of neo-Cartesianism, and there is as great a need as ever for the light of philosophical reflection to be turned into the corners where lurks the haunting shade.

Ryle's second chapter was entitled 'Knowing That and Knowing How'. The distinction between these two types of knowledge has, unlike some of Ryle's other distinctions, become a philosophical commonplace; and the chapter of *The Concept of Mind* in any case ranged more widely than its title suggested. I have, accordingly, retitled my second chaper 'Body, Soul, Mind, and Spirit'.

My third and fourth chapters bear the same titles, and cover the same topics, as Ryle's corresponding chapters: they are entitled 'The Will' and 'Emotion'. Ryle's chapters were generally recognized as two of the most successful in *The Concept of Mind*, and though my own approach to the topics differs from Ryle's, and is by implication critical of his approach, they both seek to build upon his insights.

Ryle's fifth chapter was entitled 'Dispositions and Occurrences'. This chapter, whether deliberately or unconsciously, drew to the attention of philosophers of mind the importance of some distinctions which had been emphasized by Aristotle but ignored or despised by modern philosophers. It was, in my view, the most important chapter in the book; but it also underestimated the richness of the Aristotelian battery of distinctions. Accordingly, my corresponding chapter has the fuller title 'Abilities, Faculties, Powers, and Dispositions'.

In his sixth chapter Ryle critically examined some philosophical misconceptions about the nature of self-knowledge. In the course of doing so he also exposed, by implication, some of the philosophical illusions involved in the very notion of a self. The title of my own sixth chapter, 'Self and Self-Knowledge' makes more explicit the nature of both Ryle's and my own critique.

The seventh, eighth, and ninth chapters of this book bear the same titles, and treat of roughly the same topics, as those of Ryle's book; though the philosophical account of these topics— sensation, imagination, and intellect—exhibits a much greater difference from Ryle's account than do the earlier chapters of the book. Ryle's inclination towards behaviourism was, I believe, much more damaging to his account of the imagination and the intellect than it was to his account of the emotions and the will.

The final chapter of this book, like the final chapter of Ryle's, bears the title 'Psychology'. The title does not perfectly fit the content of my Chapter 10 any more than it fitted the content of Ryle's Chapter 10. In neither case is there any attempt to give a systematic treatment or evaluation of recent empirical invest- igation into the nature of the mind. Rather, in each case, there is an attempt to show in what sense philosophy can provide foundations for, or set limits to, the scientific study of the mind.

This book, like Ryle's book, is written within the tradition of analytic philosophy. The philosophical method of each book can be described as, in a certain sense, linguistic. In the last half- century many people have described themselves as adherents of, and many people have described themselves as enemies of, linguistic philosophy. Neither adherence nor opposition is a very useful stance unless one makes clear what one means by calling a particular style of philosophy 'linguistic' .

'Philosophy is linguistic' may mean at least six different things. (1) The study of language is a useful philosophical tool. (2) It is the only philosophical tool. (3) Language is the only subject-matter of philosophy. (4) Necessary truths are estab- lished by linguistic convention. (5) Man is fundamentally a language-using animal. (6) Everyday language has a status of privilege over technical and formal systems. These six pro- positions are independent of each other. (1) has been accepted in practice by every philosopher since Plato. Concerning the other five, philosophers have been and are divided, including philo- sophers within the analytic tradition. In my own opinion, (1) and (5) are true, and the other four false. But I do not argue for this sweeping generalization anywhere in the present book.

Ryle, though a linguistic philosopher in at least one sense, did not call his book *The Language of Mind*. In my view, his book dealt not just with the language of mind, nor with the concept of mind, but with the nature of mind; though, of course, it was a philosophical and not an empirical study of that nature: a study, perhaps, of the essence of mind.

I thought of calling my own book *The Essence of Mind* but in the end I decided to entitle it, with deliberate ambiguity, *The Metaphysics of Mind*. The book is, like Ryle's, intended as a sustained attack on a false view of the mind, the Cartesian view, which is metaphysical in the sense of that word in which it was made a term of abuse by positivists, namely, as isolating statements about mental life from any possibility of verification or falsification in the public world. But the book is devoted—as much of Ryle's was—to showing the importance of distinctions between different kinds of actuality and potentiality, distinctions which were one of the major concerns of the work of Aristotle which was the first book to bear the name *Metaphysics*. This book's purpose is to show, within the realm of the philosophy of mind, the confusion which can be generated by bad meta-physics and the clarity which is impossible without good metaphysics.

In doing this I have tried to show that an employment of the techniques of linguistic analysis can go hand in hand with a respect for traditional, and indeed ancient, concepts and theses in philosophy. Though I write as an analytical philosopher, I have tried to show that the philosophical system which I try to present is continuous with that of the medieval Aristotelianism in which I received my earliest philosophical training.

It would be impudent to try to imitate Ryle's incomparable talent for presenting philosophy in a style which combined conceptual rigour with punchy colloquialism. But I have aimed to follow his example by writing in a way which is accessible to the non-philosophical reader. I have tried to avoid unexplained jargon, unnecessary symbolism, and allusive controversy with contemporary authors. Like Ryle, I have altogether forsworn the use of footnotes. My debts to other philosophers are, I hope, adequately acknowledged in a bibliographical appendix and in my other works there cited.

Balliol
March 1989

Contents

1

Descartes' Myth

DUALISM is the idea that there are two worlds. There is the physical world which contains matter, and energy, and all the tangible contents of the universe including human bodies. Then there is another psychical world: mental events and states belong to a private world which is inaccessible to public observation. According to dualism the two separate realms of mental and physical realities interact, if at all, only in a mysterious manner that transcends the normal rules of causality and evidence.

The most impressive modern presentation of dualism was the philosophy of Descartes in the seventeenth century. Descartes was a genius of extraordinary power. His main ideas can be so concisely expressed that they could be written on the back of a postcard; and yet they were so profoundly revolutionary that they altered the course of philosophy for centuries.

If you wanted to put Descartes' main ideas on the back of a postcard you would need just two sentences: man is a thinking mind; matter is extension in motion. Everything, in Descartes system, is to be explained in terms of this dualism of mind and matter. Indeed, we owe it to Descartes that we think of mind and matter as the two great, mutually exclusive and mutually exhaustive, divisions of the universe we inhabit.

For Descartes the essential thing about human beings is that they are thinking substances. Man's whole essence is mind: in the present life our minds are intimately united with our bodies, but it is not our bodies that make us what we really are. Indeed a life is possible in which we remain essentially ourselves without having any bodies at all. The essence of mind is consciousness: one's awareness of one's own thoughts and their objects. Man is the *only* conscious inhabitant of the physical world: all other animals, according to Descartes, are merely complicated, but unconscious, machines.

For Descartes, again, matter is extension in motion. By 'extension' is meant that which has the geometrical properties of shape, size, divisibility, and so on. These are the only properties to be attributed, at a fundamental level, to matter. Descartes offered to explain all the phenomena of heat, light, colour, and sound in terms of the motion of small particles of different sizes and shapes. He was one of the first systematic exponents of the idea of modern Western science as a combination of mathematical procedures and experimental methods.

Both of the great principles of Cartesian philosophy were— we now know—false. In his own lifetime phenomena were discovered which were incapable of straightforward explanation in terms of matter in motion. The circulation of the blood and the action of the heart, as discovered by the English physician William Harvey, demanded the operation of forces for which there was no room in Descartes' system. None the less, his scientific account of the origin and nature of the world was fashionable for a century or so after his death; and his conception of animals as machines was later extended by some of his disciples who claimed, to the scandal of their contemporaries, that human beings, too, were only complicated machines.

Descartes' view of the nature of mind endured much longer than his view of matter. Indeed among educated people in the West who are not professional philosophers it is still the most widespread view of mind. Most contemporary philosophers would disown Cartesian dualism but even those who explicitly renounce it are often profoundly influenced by it.

Many people, for instance, go along with Descartes in identifying the mental realm as the realm of consciousness. They think of consciousness as an object of introspection; as something we can inwardly see when we look within ourselves. They think of it as an inessential, contingent matter that consciousness has a connection with expression in speech and behaviour. Consciousness, as they conceive it, is something to which each of us has direct access in our own case. Others, by contrast, can only infer to our conscious states by accepting our testimony or making causal inferences from our physical behaviour.

In extreme reaction to Cartesian ideas there grew up in the present century a school of behaviourists, who denied the existence of the mental realm altogether. Behaviourists maintained that when we attribute mental states or events to people we are really making roundabout statements about their actual or hypothetical bodily behaviour. A crude version of behaviourism was for long very influential among psychologists. More subtle versions of behaviourism have been espoused by philosophers also.

Behaviourism attempted to reduce mentalistic items such as belief and desire to physical dispositions for bodily movement. Painstaking attempts were made, for instance, to present belief as a bodily disposition: as a tendency, it might be, to make in certain circumstances certain sounds or marks on paper. One difficulty which stands in the way of such attempts is that the bodily movements of jaw and tongue, say, which express a German's belief that the world is round are quite different from the bodily movements by which a Frenchman expresses the same belief. It is therefore doubtful whether the belief that the world is round can be analysed as a tendency to make bodily movements. If the relevant class of bodily movements is sought to be identified as those which have equivalent meanings, it will be found that the notion of meaning presents no less difficulty for behaviourist analysis than does the notion of belief.

Both dualism and behaviourism attempt to call in doubt things which we all know to be true. Behaviourism calls in doubt things which we know very well about our own minds; dualism calls in doubt things which we know very well about other people's minds.

In its most extreme form behaviourism tries to tell me that I do not have any thoughts or feelings which I keep to myself and do not exhibit in any public way; and this I know to be false. At the very least, behaviourism tries to tell me that my consciousness of all of my own thoughts and feelings is a roundabout inference from hypotheses about my likely overt behaviour in various circumstances; and this is obviously absurd.

Dualism, on the other hand, leads to scepticism about other minds, and calls into question the consciousness of people other than myself. When I look within myself, on the Cartesian view, I see consciousness. But is it not irresponsible to generalize from my own case to that of others? I cannot look within others: it is the essence of introspection that it should be something that everyone must do for themselves. Can I make a causal deduction from other people's behaviour? No, for I cannot begin to establish a correlation between other people's consciousness and their behaviour when the first term of the correlation is in principle unobservable. Of course, I may think I observe the correlation in my own case; but it is precisely this correlation which it appears rash to generalize. On this view, I observe behaviour plus consciousness in myself, but merely behaviour in others. The sample which I observe is ridiculously small to permit any extrapolation.

Fortunately, dualism and behaviourism do not exhaust the alternatives open to the student of the philosophy of mind. The most significant philosopher of mind in the twentieth century was Ludwig Wittgenstein: and Wittgenstein thought that both dualists and behaviourists were victims of confusion. Wittgenstein's own position was a middle stance between dualism and behaviourism. Mental events and states, he believed, were neither reducible to their bodily expressions (as the behaviourists had argued) nor totally separable from them (as the dualists had concluded). Even when we think our most private and spiritual thoughts, he argued, we do so through the medium of a language which is essentially tied to its public and bodily expression. Unlike the behaviourists, Wittgenstein did not deny the possibility of secret and spiritual thoughts; but on the other hand he demonstrated the incoherence of the Cartesian dichotomy of mind and body.

According to Wittgenstein the connection between mental processes and their manifestations in behaviour is not a causal connection to be discovered, like other causal connections, from the regular concomitance between these two types of events. To use Wittgenstein's technical term, the physical expression of a mental process is a *criterion* for that process: that is to say, it is part of the concept of a mental process of a particular kind that it should have a characteristic manifestation. To understand the very meaning of words such as 'pain' or 'grief' one must know that pain and grief are characteristically linked to particular bodily expressions. To understand the notion of some particular mental state, one has to understand what kinds of behaviour count as evidence for its occurrence. In these cases the relation between the behavioural evidence and the mental state is not an inductive one. That is to say, it is not the kind of connection established by the observation of the co-occurrence of two sets of independently identifiable events.

We must distinguish, Wittgenstein argued, between two kinds of evidence that we may have for the occurrence of states of affairs: we must distinguish between criteria and symptoms. Where the connection between a certain kind of evidence and the conclusion drawn from it is a matter of empirical discovery, through theory and induction, the evidence may be called a symptom of the state of affairs. Where the relation between evidence and conclusion is not something discovered by empirical investigation, but is something which must be grasped by anyone who possesses the concept of the relevant kind of thing, then the evidence is not a mere symptom, but is a criterion of the state of affairs in question. A red sky at night may be a symptom of good weather the following morning; but the absence of clouds, the shining of the sun, etc., tomorrow are not just symptoms but criteria for the good weather.

Using this distinction we can say that certain states or events in the brain may be symptoms of certain mental states but they could not be criteria for them in the way that the appropriate behaviour would be. Thus, for instance, certain electrical brain patterns may be, or may some day come to be, symptoms of the possession of a knowledge of English by the person whose brain is in question. But the person's ready use of English is not just a symptom of, it is a criterion for, his knowledge of English.

Philosophers of mind are concerned with the analysis of the relationship between mind and behaviour. When we understand, respond to, and evaluate each other's actions we make constant use of mentalistic concepts. On the basis of what people do, and in order to make sense of what they do, we attribute to them certain desires and beliefs. We ascribe their actions to choices, and we invoke, to explain their conduct, various intentions, motives, and reasons. These mentalistic concepts, such as *desire, belief, intention, motive,* and *reason,* are the subject-matter of the philosophy of mind. In human action we look for a mental element; in the philosophy of human action we study the relationship between the mental element and the overt behaviour.

Mentalistic concepts cannot be understood apart from their

function in explaining and rendering intelligible the behaviour of human agents. But this must not be misunderstood. When we explain action in terms of desires and beliefs we are not putting forward any explanatory *theory* to account for action. Though we attribute mental states and processes to people on the basis of their overt behaviour, it would be wrong to suggest that we start from direct knowledge of the physical motions of people's bodies and then frame hypotheses about the occult mental causes underlying these motions.

It is true that desires and beliefs explain action; but the explanation is not of any causal hypothetical form. It is not as if the actions of human beings constitute a set of raw data— physical motions identifiable on their faces as the kinds of actions they are—for which we then seek an explanatory hypothesis. Very often we find it much easier to give mentalistic descriptions of people's behaviour ('he was trying to open the door' 'he was threatening her') than to give precise reports of physical movements. Babies learn to respond to the moods of their parents and to guess their intentions long before they have acquired the language for giving objective physical descriptions of their parents' bodily movements.

Many things which human beings do are not identifiable as actions of a particular kind unless they are already seen and interpreted as proceeding from a particular set of desires and beliefs. Brief reflection suffices to show this in the case of such human actions as buying and selling, promising and marrying, lying and storytelling. But it can be true also of the most basic, apparently purely physical, actions, such as killing and letting die. If a witch-doctor goes through a ritual whose purpose is to cause the death of a witness if he is speaking falsehood, and if the witness then suddenly and mysteriously dies, it is much more difficult to decide whether the witch-doctor actually killed the witness than to decide what the witch-doctor's intention was.

Very often when we assign an intention to a human action, we are attributing to the agent certain reasons for action. When we say that Jane acted for a certain reason, we are attributing to her both a desire for a certain state of affairs to be brought about, and a belief that a certain manner of acting will help to bring about that state of affairs. Thus we are attributing both a cognitive and an affective state of mind.

Cognitive states of mind are those which involve a person's possession of a piece of information (true or, as the case may be, false): such things as belief, awareness, expectation, certainty, knowledge. Affective states of mind are neither true nor false but consist in an attitude of pursuit or avoidance: such things as purpose, intention, desire, volition. Some mental states, of course, are both affective and cognitive: hope and fear, for instance, involve both an expectation of a prospective state of affairs and a judgement of the state of affairs as good or evil.

When we infer in this way from behaviour and testimony to mental states and activities, we are not making a shaky inductive inference to events in an inaccessible realm. The very concepts of mental states have as their function to enable us to interpret and understand the conduct and utterances of human beings. The mind itself can be defined as the capacity for behaviour of the complicated and symbolic kinds which constitute the linguistic, social, moral, economic, scientific, cultural, and other characteristic activities of human beings in society.

The definition just suggested for the mind is very different from the Cartesian definition from which we started. For Descartes the defining characteristic of mind is consciousness rather than the capacity for symbolic activity. In order to bring out the magnitude of the Cartesian revolution in philosophy, it is worth explaining how the boundaries of the mind were drawn by him in a place quite different from that where they had been drawn by his predecessors in antiquity and in the Middle Ages, in the tradition going back to Aristotle.

For Aristotelians before Descartes the mind was essentially the faculty, or set of faculties, which set off human beings from other animals. Dumb animals and human beings shared certain abilities and activities: dogs, cows, pigs, and men could all see and hear and feel, they all had in common the faculty or faculties of sensation. But only human beings could think abstract thoughts and take rational decisions: they were marked off from the other animals by the possession of intellect and will, and it was these two faculties which essentially constituted the mind. Christian Aristotelians believed that intellectual activity was in a particular sense immaterial, whereas sensation was impossible without a material body.

For Descartes, and for the generations of philosophers and psychologists that have undergone his influence, the boundary between mind and matter was set elsewhere. It was consciousness, not intelligence or rationality, that was the defining criterion of the mental. The mind, viewed from the Cartesian standpoint, is the realm of whatever is accessible to introspection. The kingdom of the mind, therefore, included not only human understanding and willing, but also human seeing, hearing, feeling, pain, and pleasure. For every form of human sensation, according to Descartes, included an element that was spiritual rather than material, a phenomenal component which was no more than contingently connected with bodily causes, expressions, and mechanisms.

Descartes would have agreed with his Aristotelian predecessors that the mind is what distinguishes human beings from other animals. But the sense in which this thesis was true for him was quite different from the sense in which it was true for them. For them what made it true was that mind was restricted to intellect and will, and only humans had intellect and will. For him what made it true was that though mind included sensation, only humans had genuine sensation. As has been said, he denied that animals had any genuine consciousness. The bodily machinery which accompanies sensation in human beings might occur also in animal bodies; but in an animal a phenomenon like pain was a purely mechanical event, unaccompanied by the sensation which is felt by humans in pain.

The most obvious distinction between human beings and other animals appears to be that humans are language-users and other animals are not. That is why, when we want a brief way of referring to non-human animals, we call them 'dumb animals'; this, too, is one reason for the traditional definition of human beings as rational animals.

The distinction between language-users and non-language-users plays a role in both the Aristotelian and the Cartesian demarcation of the boundaries of the mind. According to the pre-Cartesian tradition the intellect in human beings is tantamount to the ability to make intelligent use of words and sentences. Descartes, too, offers humans' exclusive possession of language as a proof that only humans have minds; but unlike his predecessors he thinks that there cannot be consciousness without language. For him consciousness is the defining feature of mind, which brings linguistic ability in its train. For his predecessors the boundary between language-users and non-language-users can be drawn within the realm of conscious beings.

The reason why Descartes could use human species-specific language gifts to rule out animal consciousness was that he identified consciousness with self-consciousness. It is true that self-consciousness is not possible without language: without language there is no difference between being in pain and having the thought 'I'm in pain'. But Descartes' predecessors were right to believe that there can be consciousness without self-consciousness, and so there can be pain without language.

By introducing consciousness rather than rationality as the defining characteristic of mind, Descartes made it natural to conceive the mind as being an especially hidden and private realm.

Rationality is not something particularly private. According to Descartes' predecessors, what distinguished humans from animals was the human capacity to do such things as under-stand arithmetic and desire fame. Neither the understanding of arithmetic nor the desire for fame is a specially private state; the subject has no special authority to pronounce on their presence or absence. I may believe I understand a particular arithmetical operation, but my teacher, after a test, may show me that I do not. Similarly, it may take a perceptive friend to convince me that I am conducting a particular political campaign not out of love of justice but in order to get my name in the newspapers. In matters such as the understanding of arithmetic and the pursuit of fame my own sincere statement is not the last possible word.

On the other hand, if I want to know what sense-impressions someone is having, then I have to give his utterances a special status. The natural way to find out what someone seems to see or hear, or what he is imagining or saying to himself, is to ask him to tell me. What he says in reply need not be true—he may be insincere, or misunderstand the words he is using—but it cannot be erroneous. Experiences of this kind seem to be exempt from doubt by the person whose experiences they are.

Descartes took this kind of indubitability as the characteristic property of thought. Such experiences are private to their owner in the sense that while others can doubt them, he cannot. Privacy thus becomes a mark of the mental in the Cartesian system.

It is clear that privacy of this kind is quite distinct from rationality. The discovery of Pythagoras' theorem was an exercise of rationality, and we know this without knowing whether Pythagoras worked out the theorem first in his head or by scratching in the sand. On the other hand, mimicry of birdsong is not in itself something that exhibits rationality, whether it is done aloud or only by humming in the privacy of the imagination.

Intellection and sensation are not the only human capacities and activities which we may think of as belonging to the mind and which some philosophers have identified as mental phenomena. In addition to the ability to perceive and understand, human beings possess memory, for instance, and imagination and the passions or emotions. Descartes and his predecessors agreed in classifying memory and imagination as inner senses. They regarded these faculties as senses because they saw their function as the production of imagery, and they thought of inner imagery as a replica of outer objects of sense. They regarded these faculties as inner because their activity, unlike that of the senses, was not controlled by external stimuli.

I shall argue in a later chapter that the conception of inner senses is a mistake, and that the relationship between sensation and mental imagery was incorrectly explicated by both Descartes and his predecessors. Where Descartes differed from his predecessors, in this respect, was that he, unlike they, regarded the imagination as being part of the mind. Imagination, like sensation, was for him a mental operation which was accompanied by mechanical activity within the body. The mechanical activity of imagination—and Descartes was prepared to assign it a precise localization in the brain—was something which might take place within an animal no less than in a human being. But the pure mental activity of imagination was peculiar to humans and might take place also in a disembodied soul.

For Descartes' predecessors the imagination was not part of the mind, but was thoroughly bodily; souls and spirits who lacked bodies would similarly lack imagination. For some of Descartes' successors, on the other hand, the inner senses became the mind *par excellence*. The British empiricist philosophers, indeed, conceived of the whole relationship between mind and matter in terms of the relationship between the operation of the inner senses and the operation of the outer senses.

In the psychology of David Hume, the deliverances of the outer senses are impressions, the deliverances of the inner senses are ideas; the whole content of our minds, the phenomenal base from which the whole of the world is to be constructed, consists of nothing but impressions and ideas. Moreover, the meaning of the words of our language consists in their relation to impressions and ideas. It is the flow of impressions and ideas in our minds which makes our utterances not empty sounds, but the expression of thought; and if a word cannot be shown to refer to an impression or to an idea it must be discarded as meaningless.

The empiricist account of the relation between language and thought is perverse. The question whether there can be thought without imagery is not a simple one, and later in this book I shall try to unravel some of its complexity. But even if we grant, for the sake of argument, that thought and imagination often go hand in hand, it is important to be clear which of these operations confers meaning on which. In fact, when we think in images it is thought that confers meaning on the images and not vice versa. When we talk silently to ourselves, the words we utter in imagination would not have the meaning they do were it not for our intellectual mastery of the language to which they belong. And when we think in visual images as well as in unuttered words, the images merely provide the illustration to a text whose meaning is given by the words which express the thoughts.

An empiricist philosopher might be willing to accept the claim that images possess the meaning they do only when they are in the mind of a language-user. But he might maintain that the mastery of language is something which is itself to be explained in terms of laws of association between images in succession. But this seems to be a mistake. Language acquisition can only be explained if we postulate a special ability specific to the human race. Domestic animals live in the same sensory environment as human babies, yet seem unable to achieve the mastery of abstract and universal terms which the child acquires as it grows. If we are willing to talk of inner senses at all, we must no doubt attribute them to animals no less than to humans; but for language acquisition both the Aristotelian and Cartesian traditions would insist that an inner sense was not enough, an intellect was necessary. In the empiricist account of mind previous philosophers would have failed to recognize anything which they would call the intellect. The empiricist programme might indeed be described as the endeavour to eliminate the intellect in favour of the inner sense.

In the last two decades there has been a surprising revival of Cartesianism. This has been due principally to two factors: first, to an insufficient understanding by philosophers of the conclusiveness of the death-blow dealt to the notion of Cartesian consciousness by Wittgenstein's philosophical critique; and secondly, to the revival of certain other aspects of Descartes' philosophy by the linguist Noam Chomsky.

One of Descartes' theories was that some of the ideas which played a crucial role in human understanding were not acquired through experience but were an innate part of the structure of the mind. This thesis was bitterly opposed by the empiricist philosophers who followed Descartes, and in much of nineteenth- and twentieth-century psychology it was taken for granted that on this matter Descartes was wrong and the empiricists were right.

Chomsky, by contrast, defended the Cartesian tradition as the best framework for the understanding of human use of language. The data presented to an infant, Chomsky argued, are too fragmentary to provide a basis for language to be acquired by any of the normal procedures of learning; the swift mastery of language by children can only be explained on the basis of a species-specific innate human ability.

Chomsky's theory, at least in its initial form, was an empirical hypothesis. He claimed that the mind possesses innately certain organizing principles of universal grammar as an abstract system underlying behaviour. The existence or non-existence of such a model was to be argued for in terms of its necessity or adequacy in explaining certain human linguistic activities and skills (in particular the construction of well-formed sentences of varying degrees of complexity).

Not all Chomsky's readers have been convinced that the innate structures of mind postulated by his linguistic theory have more than the name in common with Descartes' innate ideas. Indeed, much of Chomsky's theoretical apparatus would have been severely frowned upon by Descartes. For instance, Chomsky reintroduced the notion of *faculty* and gave it an importance in psychology which it had not had for many centuries. He distinguished, for example, between the language-faculty and the number-faculty, and claimed that the phenomena of human language acquisition showed that there must be a species-specific language-faculty quite distinct from a capacity for mathematical computation which might be common not only to human beings but to other species on other planets who would be baffled by anything similar to human language. Descartes, on the other hand, regarded the notion of faculties as an Aristotelian anachronism which stood in the way of genuine scientific progress.

Again, Chomsky believed that in using language we display tacit knowledge, operating rules and principles that cannot in the normal way be brought to conscious formulation. Descartes, who defined the contents of the mind in terms of consciousness, would have been obliged to reject any appeal to tacit, unformulated knowledge.

None the less, Chomsky's patronage of Cartesian linguistics gave new life to many Cartesian philosophical ideas. In particular, the notion of Cartesian consciousness, which many philosophers thought had been killed by the work of Wittgenstein, rose from the dead in the most remarkable manner. This revival was dignified by some commentators as the 'mentalist revolution' of the 1970s.

There is nothing philosophically objectionable in Chomsky's postulation of innate mental structures. Obviously, human beings are born with certain abilities, including abilities to mature as well as abilities to learn. Whether the ability to acquire grammars of a certain kind is an ability to learn or an ability to mature under certain conditions is a philosophically open question capable of being settled by empirical enquiry.

Again, the notion of *faculty* did not ever deserve the obloquy into which it fell during several centuries. Of course if a faculty is thought of as an immaterial organ, or as a paramechanical impulse, the notion offers itself to destructive philosophical parody. But if by a faculty we simply mean a particular kind of mental ability, then it is beyond doubt that human beings have various faculties. The philosophical notion of faculty will be analysed sympathetically in Chapter 5 of this book.

But it is a remarkable thing that the Cartesian notion of consciousness has returned to favour, among some admirers of Chomsky, on the coat-tails of the Cartesian notion of innate ideas and the very non-Cartesian notion of faculties. It is common for us now to be told that mental states, in addition to whatever relationships they may have to bodily inputs or outputs, have an inner or qualitative nature which is fundamentally inexpressible. In the case of sensations these are called 'sensory qualia'. Pains, for instance, have an intrinsic quality which is revealed in introspection, which is quite distinct from any of the criteria for pain which might be ascertainable by an external observer. Any adequate philosophy of mind, we are told, must be able to make room for these ineffable qualia.

The alleged existence of qualia is often held to present a difficulty for the currently most fashionable philosophy of mind which is called 'functionalism'. Functionalism is popular not only among philosophers and psychologists but also among researchers in artificial intelligence and in cognitive science. Students of artificial intelligence aim to produce computers that will not just solve problems but solve them in the way that human beings do. In relation to ordinary computer designers and programmers they may be compared with aeronautic engineers who are concerned not to devise the most efficient aeroplane, but to construct an artificial bird. Devotees of 'cognitive science' may operate in a number of different disciplines—philosophy, empirical psychology, artificial intelligence. The name is not so much the demarcation of an area of study as a manifesto of belief that the characteristic features of human mentality will eventually be explicable in demythologized form by certain fashionable scientific procedures.

Functionalism is often presented as a sophisticated modification of behaviourism. Whereas behaviourism thought that each mental state could be defined in terms of its behavioural expression, or its behavioural output in conjunction with its environmental input, functionalism accepts that mental states cannot be defined except in relation to other mental states. According to functionalism, what will be defined in terms of external input and observable output, even on the most optimistic view, will not be individual mental states, but only the network of interrelated mental states and processes which constitute the natural history of the mind.

Though many functionalists accept, with various degrees of reluctance, the existence of inexpressible qualia in human beings, the reference to 'function' in the title of their philosophical allegiance is meant to emphasize that what is important in mental states is not their inward feel but their external input–output relationship. The crucial element in mentality, functionalists maintain, is neither the felt quality of mental states, nor the hardware in which the mental states are embodied, but the structure of the mental activities which the hardware supports.

In this, functionalism incorporates an important truth. Human beings are creatures of flesh and blood with certain abilities which constitute their minds. There is nothing in the nature of the human mind which means that it could not be incarnate, or rather enmattered, in creatures with quite different physical constitutions. Moreover, even in the case of humans of flesh and blood, there is nothing in the nature of our minds which proves to us that we are not extremely skilful artefacts.

From time to time I entertain the fantasy that one day there will be a knock on the door, and a technician will introduce himself saying: 'I have come from IBM, sir, to give you your mid-life service.' Of course I know that this is an absurd fantasy. But I know that I am not a man-made computer only in the same way as I know that cats do not grow on trees. I know this not by any argument 'I think, therefore I am not an artefact'.

If I am sceptical about the types of claim made at the present time by cognitive scientists and experts in artificial intelligence it is not because I think that there is an a priori argument which shows that no computer could ever be conscious or have a mind. It is certainly not because I believe, as Descartes did, that there is a realm of consciousness which is totally divorced from the physical world in which software is designed and hardware is manufactured. It is for exactly the opposite reason: it is because I think that the heredity of Descartes prevents those who work in these fields from really understanding the problem they are intending to solve, the mental structure they are intending to emulate. It is for this reason that I believe that it is, once again, worth while to attempt to destroy the Cartesian myth.

2

Body, Soul, Mind, and Spirit

DESCARTES, in sceptical vein, believed that he could doubt the existence of the external world and the existence of his own body. He brought his doubt to an end with the argument 'Cogito, ergo sum'—'I think, therefore I am'. This led to the question 'What am I?' Descartes' answer was that he was a substance whose whole essence or nature was to think, and whose being required no place and depended on no material thing. This answer encapsulates the erroneous dualism discussed in the last chapter.

To Descartes' question 'What am I?' my own answer is that I am a human being, a living body of a certain kind. We sometimes speak as if we have bodies, rather than are bodies. But having a body, in this natural sense, is not incompatible with being a body; it does not mean that there is something other than my body which *has my* body. Just as my body has a head, a trunk, two arms, and two legs, but is not something over and above the head, trunk, arms, and legs, so I have a body but am not something over and above the body. As well as a body I have a mind: that is to say, I have various psychological capacities, including especially an intellect and a will.

To say that I have an intellect is to say that I have the capacity to acquire and exercise intellectual abilities of various kinds, such as the mastery of language and the possession of objective information. To say that I have a will is to say that I have the capacity for the free pursuit of goals formulated by the intellect. My intellect and my will are in essence capacities. What are they capacities *of* ? Of the living human being, the body you would see if you were here in the room where I write.

You who are reading this book likewise have a body and a mind. You have a mind, as is proved by the fact that you can read and understand what I have written. You have a body: the body in which are the eyes with which you are reading this

book, or the ears which are hearing it read to you. Every other
reader of this book too has a body and a mind. That human
beings in general have minds and bodies—that is to say that
they are bodies with certain psychological capacities—is simply
a truism.

Is it similarly a truism to say that human beings have souls?
That depends on how one understands the word 'soul'.
Understood in one way, to say that an animal has a soul is to say
something more than to say that it has a mind. Understood in
another way, it is to say something very much less.

When they say that human beings have souls, philosophers
and theologians often mean something more than just that
human beings have minds (intellects and wills). They mean that
human beings have immortal minds: minds which can survive
the death of the bodies whose minds they are, minds which can
live without bodies at least for a period and perhaps for ever.
This claim is supported sometimes by philosophical argument,
sometimes by appeal to religious revelation, sometimes by
alleging communication from those beyond the grave. I do not
wish to discuss here the plausibility of the evidence offered in
support of immortality. I want merely to mark the great
difference between this controversial claim that human beings
have souls and the truism that human beings have minds.

Philosophers in the tradition of Aristotle used the Greek and
Latin words corresponding to 'soul' not to mean something
more than an intellect, but to mean something less. By 'soul'
Aristotle simply meant 'principle of life', in such a way that all
living things by definition had souls. If one understands 'soul'
in this way, then not only human beings have souls, but also
animals and even plants. And there is no presumption that
souls are necessarily immaterial: the soul of a plant might turn
out to be a string of DNA. According to the Aristotelian
tradition, if the human soul turns out, on philosophical
investigation, to be immaterial and immortal, that is because of
something special to humanity, not because of something
proper to souls as such.

Given the history of the English word 'soul' it would be
misleading to say that plants have souls. It would suggest that
one thought they had some kind of consciousness, or that they
could respond when one talks to them. It sounds less strange to

attribute souls to animals; but outside the Aristotelian context this too could be misleading, suggesting that one was attributing immortality to one's pets, looking forward perhaps to reunion with them in some doggy heaven or happy hunting ground. To avoid these possible misunderstandings, I shall use the word 'soul' only in the theological sense in which it has come to be the equivalent of 'immortal mind'.

The mind, I have said, includes the intellect and the will. Do the intellect and the will constitute the mind, or are there other human capacities which are part of the mind? What of the senses and the imagination? In Chapter 1 I explained how according to the pre-Cartesian view of the mind the senses were not part of the mind; and I have taken sides with the Aristotelian tradition which regards the intellect as the mind *par excellence*. However, I rejected the view, common to both pre- and post-Cartesian philosophers, that the imagination was a kind of sense. At this point I wish to reserve judgement on the question whether the imagination is part of the mind. The question will be discussed in Chapter 8.

Now though the senses are not part of the mind, they are undoubtedly psychological capacities; indeed a large part of psychology consists in the study of the operation of the senses and the physiological mechanisms which underlie them. We may wish to have a word to refer to the cluster of sensory capacities in the way in which 'mind', in my usage, refers to the cluster of capacities whose major members are the intellect and the will. The most appropriate word seems to be 'psyche'. If we adopt this usage we can say that whereas on earth only humans have minds, humans and other animals have psyches.

Having thus delimited the psyche, let us set it aside for the moment to concentrate on the mind. All of us, at one time or another, are inclined to think of the mind as an inner landscape, a more or less mysterious region which needs to be explored and mapped. In this chapter I wish to evaluate philosophically this metaphor: to ask whether, in prosaic truth, there is an inner region within each of us for us to explore.

The boundaries of the mind, as we have seen in Chapter 1, are placed in different places by different philosophers. The geography of the mind is not a simple matter to discover, because its most basic features are a matter of dispute between philosophers. It cannot be explored simply by looking within ourselves at an inward landscape laid out to view. What we see when we take this inner look will be partly determined by the philosophical viewpoint from which we look, or, we might say, by the conceptual spectacles we may be wearing.

In this chapter I will start from the definition of mind which was suggested in the previous one. The mind, I said, can be defined as the capacity for behaviour of the complicated and symbolic kinds which constitute the linguistic, social, moral, economic, scientific, cultural, and other characteristic activities of human beings in society.

In its primary sense the human mind is the capacity to acquire intellectual abilities. It is a capacity, not an activity: babies have minds even though they do not yet exhibit intellectual activities. It is a second-order capacity: an ability to acquire or possess abilities. To know a language is to have an ability: the ability to speak, understand, and perhaps read the language. To have a mind is to have a capacity one stage further back: the ability to acquire abilities such as the knowledge of a language.

Human beings are not born with knowledge of language: they learn languages as they develop. This is true, whether or not the learning of language by human beings is something which can only be explained if we postulate certain innate tendencies or structures. It is conceivable that there could be beings who spoke language from birth. It would surely be wrong to deny that they had minds, on the grounds that they did not have the capacity to *acquire* knowledge of language. So while the human mind is the capacity to acquire intellectual abilities, mind as such is the capacity to possess intellectual abilities.

The most important intellectual skill is the mastery of language. Others, such as knowledge of mathematics, are acquired by human beings through the languages they have mastered. So the study of the acquisition and exercise of language is the way *par excellence* to study the nature of the human mind. To study knowledge of language you have to consider what the exercise of linguistic knowledge is. The exercise of linguistic knowledge is linguistic behaviour: but 'behaviour' here must be understood broadly, so that, for instance, reciting a poem to myself in my head imperceptibly will count as an instance of linguistic behaviour.

If the mind is the capacity to acquire intellectual abilities, what is the nature of the will? Traditionally the intellect and the will stood side by side as the two great faculties of the mind. Traditionally, too, the will is thought of as the locus of autonomy: of the human agent's possession of personal, long-term ideals. These features of the traditional picture fit well with our definition. The pursuit of self-selected goals that go beyond the immediate environment in space and time is not possible without the use of symbols for the distant, the remote, and the universal. And on the other hand, the use of symbols itself involves purposes which go beyond the temporal and spatial present. First of all, meaning something is a matter of intending, and intending involves having purposes: again, meaning is done in accordance with rules, and rules are of their nature capable of repeated application in diverse circumstances. Secondly, to use something as a symbol and not as a tool is to use it in such a way that any effect which it may have on the environment lacks the immediacy and regularity characteristic of physical causality. So the mind, as the capacity for intellectual abilities, is a volitional as well as a cognitive capacity, includes the will as well as the intellect.

The contrast between cognitive and affective, in human life, cuts across the demarcation between the life of the senses and the life of the mind. At the purely animal level of sensation there are both perceptions and feelings, just as at the mental level there is the distinction between intellect and will. Moreover, just as in human beings the operation of the senses is shot through with the conceptualizations of the intellect, so the will is, to a greater or lesser degree, in control of our animal as well as our mental life.

We cannot, of course, choose what we see when we open our eyes. But we can choose whether to open or shut them and in which direction to look with our open eyes. All the sense-organs are to some extent subject to voluntary control and therefore to the imperium of volition. The operation of the imagination, unruly though it may be, is likewise under voluntary control: it may be difficult to prevent ourselves brooding on an injury, or to banish disgusting fantasies, but, given sufficient effort it can be done. It is no more difficult than to control obsessive actions in the outer world, such as keeping one's tongue away from a sore tooth or preventing oneself from itching at a scab.

The operation of the intellect itself is not in the same way under voluntary control. Looking up at the flashing lights of the advertisements in Piccadilly Circus, one cannot prevent oneself from understanding their message. (How much more beautiful they would be, G. K. Chesterton once remarked, if only one could not read!). Nor can one, simply by stiffening one's resolve, believe fifty impossible things before breakfast.

Indirectly, of course, one's understanding and one's belief are under voluntary control: one can make oneself understand certain things by taking a course in French, and if one reads only the right newspapers and talks only to the right people one will no doubt reach the right—by the appropriate definition—political beliefs.

But if the will can, in this way, control the intellect, the will itself is at the mercy of the intellect. For the will is the capacity for rational desire; and the will can only pursue what the intellect can understand. The mind—considered as intellect and will together—is, if all goes well, supreme in the human soul; but neither intellect nor will is an autocratic emperor; rather, they are joint consuls on the model of the Roman Republic.

My definition of mind differs in two ways from some familiar ones. First, I do not take the making and use of tools as in itself an exhibition of mentality. To use inert instruments in the performance of an activity may or may not be a manifestation of mind. Whether it is or not will depend largely on what the activity is. Using a clock to tell the time or a sharp flint to carve pictures on a rock is an intellectual activity. But the use of a bamboo pole as a bridge across a stream, or the use of a stalk to collect termites, is not in the same way an indication of intellect.

Secondly, in my definition of mind I have not said anything about consciousness. To explain why, I should distinguish three different things which might be meant by 'consciousness'.

First, one might mean Cartesian consciousness: the feature that is common to, and peculiar to, the contents of the private world of introspection. This, I would argue, is a piece of philosophical nonsense. For if 'consciousness' is the name for something which can be observed only by introspection, then the meaning of this name must be learnt by a private and uncheckable performance. But no word could acquire a meaning by such a performance; for a word only has meaning as part of a language; and a language is essentially something public and shared. How do I know on this view that what I have christened by the name 'consciousness' is what you have christened by this name? And if I have not given a word a meaning which I can communicate to anyone else, I have not given it a meaning at all.

Secondly, 'consciousness' may mean the exercise of our capacities for perception: the awareness of, and ability to respond to, changes in the environment which are given us by the senses like hearing, seeing, smelling, and tasting. Consciousness in this sense is not a philosopher's *Unding*, but an important feature of the world. It is not, however, a defining feature of mind, if mind is what distinguishes human beings from other animals. For consciousness in this sense is shared by cats and dogs and cows and sheep no less than by human beings.

Thirdly, distinct from 'consciousness' in this sense there is the consciousness that is self-consciousness: the consciousness of what one is doing and undergoing, and why. In human beings self-consciousness presupposes sense-consciousness, but it is not identical with it, because it presupposes also the possession of language. One cannot think about oneself without being able to talk about oneself, and one cannot know how to talk about oneself without knowing how to talk.

This last does not depend on any general thesis that thinking involves talking: it rests on a particular reason linking thought about oneself with talk about oneself. A dog may think that he is about to be fed; but without language he cannot think that he is thinking that he is about to be fed. There is nothing in his behavioural repertoire to express the difference between the thoughts 'I am about to be fed' and 'I am thinking that I am about to be fed'. If self-consciousness is thus intimately connected with language, then one can do justice to the tradition which regards self-consciousness as an essential element of mentality, without explicitly including it in the definition.

What, now, is the relation between senses and intellect? How are these faculties which we have distinguished interrelated with each other? Broadly speaking, the senses provide us with experience, the intellect provides us with concepts. Both concepts and experience are needed for human beings to understand and cope with the world in which they live.

In order to possess a concept of something which can be an object of experience, it is not sufficient simply to have the appropriate experience. Young children see coloured objects before they painfully acquire colour-concepts; dumb animals can see and taste a substance such as salt but they cannot acquire the concepts which language-users can exercise in general judgements about salt. A special ability unshared by animals is necessary if human beings are to acquire concepts from the experience which they share with animals. Animals share with human beings the experience of pain, and human beings *feel* pain from birth and before; but we acquire the *concept* pain when we learn language. Again, rats can see, and discriminate between circles and triangles; but no amount of gazing at diagrams will make a rat a student of geometry. The intellect is the ability, confined so far as we know to the human species, to bring the experiences of the senses under universal concepts and make general and objective judgements about them.

My claim that the intellect is peculiar to the human species is not meant to be the enunciation of a philosophically necessary truth. The philosophical truth is that the intellect is the ability to acquire languages of the kind that human beings acquire. It is a matter of empirical fact whether only human beings possess this ability.

In recent years researchers have claimed that animals other than humans, such as dolphins and apes, also possess the ability to master language. The most impressive reports concern two famous chimpanzees, Washoe and Sarah.

Washoe was brought up, almost as if she were a human child, in an American family who trained her in Ameslan, a language of hand gestures used by the deaf. Her trainers claimed that she acquired a vocabulary of about 160 words, which she would on occasion put together into sentences. When grown up, she appeared to use some of the signs for communication with other chimpanzees who had been similarly trained.

Sarah was trained in a different kind of language whose 'words' were magnetic coloured plastic symbols, which could be formed into 'sentences' by being placed on metal surfaces. Her trainers claimed that she learned the use of nouns, verbs, function words such as the negation sign and the conditional 'if–then', and highly abstract words such as 'same' and 'different'.

It was and continues to be disputed whether the achievements of Washoe and Sarah amounted to genuine use of language. Linguists who studied the record of their performance denied that they showed any genuine mastery of syntax. Devotees of the chimpanzees claimed that their performance compared favourably with two-year-old children. Sceptics replied that the noises made by two-year-olds are regarded as inchoate language only because of what the children will later go on to do when they reach a stage of sophistication which the chimpanzees never reached.

The debate is an interesting one, and will no doubt continue whether or not further empirical evidence is obtained of unusual ability on the part of chimpanzees. However, there is no need for the purposes of this book to take sides in this debate. As said above, the link between language and mind is a matter of philosophy; the question whether non-human species can master language is a matter for scientific enquiry. For my part, I am convinced by the arguments of those who say that Washoe and Sarah did not show genuine mastery of language. But those who take the opposite view need not put the book down at this point. Only, whenever in future I talk of 'humans' they should interpret this as meaning 'language-using animals'; and when I talk of 'animals' they should interpret this as meaning 'non-language using animals'. For all the arguments which are used in the book are compatible with agnosticism about the possibility of animals acquiring genuine language.

It may be argued that the definition of the mind as an intellectual capacity is too austere and abstract. Some may feel that it is a perverse denial of the reality of the mind. Surely the mind is not just a faculty: it is an immaterial and private world, the locus of our secret thoughts, the auditorium of our interior monologues, the theatre in which our dreams are staged and our plans rehearsed. To define the mind as a capacity is, it may be urged, to ignore all this: it is a dogmatic behaviouristic failure to look the obvious in the eye.

Now it would be folly to deny that human beings can keep their thoughts secret, can talk to themselves without making any noise, can sketch figures before their mind's eye instead of on pieces of paper. But the capacity for mental imagery of this kind—visual, audio-motor, and other imagery—is not the intellect, or mind, but a quite different faculty. We may call it 'imagination', in one of the varied senses of that word—the ability to phantasize, to produce mental imagery.

Imagination, so understood, is, no less than the mind, a

capacity or faculty. Particular exercises of the imaginative fancy are psychological events, occurring at particular times and places; they are experiences, in relation to which the subject is in a uniquely authoritative position. These psychological events occur with great frequency in our lives; they may play a greater or lesser part in our lives according to the active or contemplative nature of our temperament and vocation.

There is a perfectly natural use of the word 'mental' in which exercises of the imaginative fancy may be called 'mental events'. When children are asked to work out arithmetical problems 'in their head' rather than on paper, they are said to be doing 'mental arithmetic'. But this sense of 'mental', though natural, may be misleading. What proves that children have minds is that they can learn to do arithmetic at all; being able to do the working in interior monologue is a comparatively unimportant extra. Doing a difficult sum on paper may be a greater proof of intellect than doing an easy one in the head. It is the nature of the skill exercised that is the crucial matter; the ability to exercise it silently and motionlessly is an added grace, no more.

Just as mental utterances are no more intellectual than overt utterances, similarly there is no reason to regard them as being endowed with a special and inescapable sincerity. We can be insincere when we talk to ourselves in silence no less than when we talk to others aloud. This is something which has long been familiar to novelists.

To illustrate this we may utilize a striking passage in Trollope's novel *Rachel Ray*. Miss Pucker, the killjoy evangelical Christian, has constantly represented the attentions which the hero, Luke Rowan, pays to the heroine, Rachel Ray, as dishonourable trifling. But as the novel reaches its conclusion, the evidence mounts up that he seriously intends to marry her. Miss Pucker sees him, one day, walking towards the heroine's house.

'If that ain't young Rowan going out to Bragg's End again!' she said to herself, comforting herself, I fear, or striving to comfort herself, with an inward assertion that he was not going there for any good. Striving to comfort herself, but not effectually; for though the assertion was made by herself to herself, yet it was not believed. Though she declared, with well-pronounced mental words, that Luke Rowan was going on that path for no good purpose, she felt a wretched conviction at her heart's core that Rachel Ray would be made to triumph over her and her early suspicions by a happy marriage. (World's Classics edition, Oxford, 1988, p. 375.)

Mental words no less than public utterances may be at some distance from the heart's core.

Just as the expression 'mental arithmetic' may mislead, so may the description of sums as done 'in the head'. The mental events which are exercises of the fancy occur at particular times and places; a child may do a piece of mental arithmetic while he is sitting at his desk, just as he may see a sparrow while running in the playground. If we say that he did the arithmetic 'in his head' this does not give a further localization which is more precise than the localization 'at his desk'.

The head is the locus of the imagination only in this sense: that the things we imagine ourselves doing are often things which we do quite literally with our heads or parts of them. When we talk to ourselves silently we imagine ourselves talking; and talking is done with the tongue, lips, and palate, so that the imagined talking is felt in those and connected areas. Of course, in doing mental arithmetic we use our brains; but that is not why we speak of mental arithmetic as done 'in the head', because we use our brains no less when we do arithmetic on paper.

Philosophers and psychologists have devoted much thought and investigation to answering the question 'Where is the mind localized?' Ancient thinkers, we are often told, regarded the heart or the liver as the organ of thought; now we know better and realize that the cerebral cortex is the seat of the higher human capacities. The operation of different senses can be assigned to different regions of the cortex; the question that remains for exploration is whether intellectual functions can be similarly given a precise location.

However, it cannot be taken for granted that the question about the localization of the mind and its faculties has a single clear sense. A capacity is not, in the ordinary sense of the words, something which occupies space at all. My front-door key is either in the lock or not in the lock; but its ability to fit the lock (which it has whether or not it is actually in the lock) is not something which can be similarly assigned to a particular place. My car's capacity to do 120 m.p.h. is something which it would be foolish to look for under the bonnet, as one might look for the carburettor under the bonnet.

Now the mind and its faculties are capacities and therefore my mind cannot be given a straightforward location as my body can. When my body is in a particular place, say on the summit of the Matterhorn, my mind is not in that place except in the sense that that is where the body is whose mind it is. To think that the mind was literally located in the brain would be as gross an error as to think that it is located in the heart or the liver.

However, there are ways in which we can localize capacities without absurdity. One way is to localize a capacity by pointing to the place, or part, where the organism or mechanism exercises its capacity. In this sense my capacity to kneel is localized in my knees and my capacity to smell is localized in my nose. (My capacity to stand is not in quite the same way localized in my legs and feet, since, with some training, I can stand on my hands or my head as well.) In this sense one cannot localize the intellect in any particular part of the body, for every part of the body that is subject to voluntary control is capable of being used in behaviour manifesting intelligence. Handicapped people learn to paint with their feet or to write by holding pens between their teeth; and very intelligent thoughts have been expressed by people who could only communicate by operating a prosthesis with minute jerks of the head.

Another way in which capacities can be localized is by finding which parts of their possessors are necessary conditions for their exercise. This localization includes, but is not necessarily exhausted by, the localization in the first sense. My key's ability to fit the front-door lock resides in the wards of its bit, in both the first and the second senses. But my car's ability to travel fast, though localized in the wheels in the first sense, cannot be precisely localized in the second sense at all, since many different parts of the engine and transmission must be in good condition if it is to be able to travel at peak velocity. Similarly, if I am to be able to kneel I need not only a pair of knees, but muscles and nerves in working order.

Psychologists who have sought to localize the mind have often done so by seeking structures and areas which were necessary conditions for the exercise of mental capacities. They have correlated the occurrence of lesions in certain parts of the brain with particular deficits in intellectual performance. Thus, in the nineteenth century the French surgeon Broca discovered that patients who had lost the ability to speak frequently had injuries in a particular area of the left frontal lobe of the brain. This has been taken as evidence that the faculty of speech is localized in the left-hand side of the brain. Later Wernicke discovered that aphasia was also correlated with lesions further back, in the left temporal lobe. However, the types of aphasia which are characteristic of lesions in Wernicke's area differ from those associated with lesions in Broca's area. In Broca's aphasia the patient has difficulty in finding uncommon words and names, while commonly retaining a good grasp of the meaning of the function words that structure sentences. In Wernicke's aphasia the patient is, by contrast, fluent, but the stream of words emitted does not constitute meaningful sentences. Here, then, we have two highly specific deficits in intellectual performance correlated with lesions in precisely determined parts of the brain; deficits which may or may not be accompanied with concomitant disorders of reading, writing, and understanding.

If we say that this proves that the faculty of speech is localized in the left hemisphere of the brain, what we really mean is that—in the normal case—the healthy functioning of the left hemisphere is a necessary condition for a human being to exercise the ability to speak. But the localization—in this sense—does not seem to be universal. People whose left hemispheres are damaged in infancy can learn to speak perfectly adequately, and left-handed people can retain the ability to speak intact even if the left hemisphere suffers injury.

Some philosophers and psychologists appear to believe that faculties can be localized in a much stronger sense than this. That is to say, they believe that the condition of the brain, or of a particular area of it, may be both a necessary *and sufficient* condition for the occurrence of particular mental events. In support of this contention they would appeal to experiments of the following kinds.

The Canadian surgeon Wilder Penfield stimulated the surface of the brain of conscious patients with mild electric currents. Stimulation of one area of the brain—the touch area—led to the patient reporting strange skin sensations; stimulation of another area—the visual cortex—led to the patient reporting flashes of light. Most strikingly, stimulation of the temporal lobe led to reports of very specific mental events: of hearing a mother calling her child many years ago, of hearing carnival voices and seeing circus wagons.

If one takes a Cartesian view of vision and memory, thinking of these two faculties as being essentially the capacity to experience private mental events, then one will quite naturally take experiments of this kind as showing that brain stimulation is not only necessary but sufficient to produce events of the appropriate kind. One may well then go on to conclude that vision is located in the visual cortex, memory in the temporal lobe, perhaps specifically in the hippocampus.

If one is not a Cartesian, one will be more cautious in taking the reports of patients at their face value as evidence of the occurrence of particular mental events. In later chapters, on sensation and imagination, I will try to show what a non-Cartesian would regard as the appropriate philosophical framework for the understanding of such phenomena.

For the moment I wish merely to stress that in all of these cases of localization the reason for believing that certain mental events are taking place, or that certain mental skills have been impaired, has nothing to do with the fact that the brain is in a certain condition or is being stimulated in a certain way. The criteria by which the investigator judges that certain mental events are taking place, or certain intellectual abilities are lacking, are the normal behavioural ones: what the patient says and does, or fails to be able to say and do.

Some philosophers and psychologists carry their enthusiasm for localizing the mind to such an extent that they will claim that the mind can be simply identified with the brain. Such an identification can be shown in two ways to be totally misguided. First, there can be brains without minds: a human brain which has spent all its life in a vat cannot have thoughts and therefore does not have a mind, no matter how similar it may be electrically and neurologically to a normal human brain. Secondly, it is conceivable that there should be minds without brains. If, when I die, it turns out that there is nothing but sawdust in my skull, that would be an astonishing miracle. But if it happened it would not cast the slightest doubt on the fact that I have a mind, which is proved beyond question by the fact that I know English and am using it to write this book.

The link between the mind and the behaviour that exhibits

mentality is a conceptual one; the link between the mind and the brain is a contingent one discovered by empirical research. The empirical research which links intellectual performance with brain function must presuppose, and cannot therefore undermine, the behavioural criteria by which we ascertain the intellectual performance which provides one term of the correlation to be established.

Behaviour is behaviour *of a body*. What does this entail when we consider whether there can be such things as bodiless minds? When I die, my body will cease to be me and I will no longer exist. Some people believe that intellectual and volitional capacities can be exercised apart from the body. I find this difficult to understand. It is true that in the present life there are intellectual and volitional activities which do not involve any bodily activity, such as silent thought and spiritual longings. No doubt even such activities depend on the activity of the brain, but this appears to be a contingent rather than a necessary truth. But it is not a merely contingent fact that the person whose thoughts and longings they are is a visible and tangible body; and I do not for my part find it easy to make sense of the idea that such activities can take place, and be attributed to individual souls, in the absence of bodies to individuate the souls. For in the sense in which it is undoubtedly true to say that I have a soul, the soul appears to be *my* soul simply and solely because it is the soul of *this* body.

I do not, however, at this point wish to take issue with those who believe in disembodied immortal souls. For what I have just said would not necessarily be rejected by those who believe in such souls. We may take St Thomas Aquinas as a spokesman for such believers. Aquinas undoubtedly believed that each human being had an immortal soul, which could survive the death of the body and continue to will and think in the period before the eventual resurrection of the body to which he looked forward. None the less, Aquinas did not believe that he could survive, as the person he was, in a self which was distinct from the body, because he did not think that disembodied souls were persons. Even after death, he believed his soul was the soul it was only because it was the soul which had been the soul of a particular body. Fully personal survival, according to him, was possible only if there was to be a resurrection of the body.

3

The Will

In modern philosophical tradition there have been two dominant conceptions of the will, one introvert and one extrovert.

In the introvert view the will is a phenomenon, an episode in one's mental history, an item of introspective consciousness. Volition is a mental event whose occurrence makes the difference between voluntary and involuntary actions. For an overt action to be voluntary is for it to be preceded and caused by a characteristic internal impression or conscious thought.

For the extrovert philosopher the correct way to study the will is to look at the observable behaviour of agents and ask for the external criteria by which to distinguish between voluntary and involuntary actions. The extrovert may see the mark of voluntariness as being a certain style of activity or, more likely, as simply the absence of certain untoward features which would render the action involuntary.

Neither the introvert nor the extrovert tradition does justice to the nature of the will.

The volitions postulated by the introvert tradition are mythical. If volitions were genuine mental events occurring with the frequency which the introvert theory demands, it should be possible for any articulate human being to answer questions about the nature, occurrence, timing, intensity and qualities. But this is notoriously not the case. Further, the introvert theory leads to a damaging regress. Volitions are postulated to be that which makes actions voluntary. However not only bodily, but also mental operations may be voluntary. So what of volitions themselves? Are they voluntary or involuntary motions of the mind? If the latter, then how can the actions that issue from them be voluntary? If the former, then in accordance with the theory they must themselves proceed from prior volitions, and those from other volitions, and so *ad infinitum*.

But the extrovert theory fails also: the distinction between voluntary and involuntary action cannot be made out simply by reference to external features or circumstances of overt behaviour. Like the introvert theory, the pure extrovert theory fails to take account of the voluntariness of purely mental operations. Mental activities may be voluntary or involuntary; but if they are not expressed in overt behaviour their voluntariness cannot consist in the features or circumstances of such behaviour.

The link between voluntariness and behaviour is to be made at the level of capacity, not of activity. The distinction between the voluntary and involuntary activity of a human agent is not a distinction between different ways of behaving; but the difference between the kinds of agent which can act voluntarily (e.g. humans) and the kinds of agent which can not (e.g. pebbles) is a difference in behavioural capacity.

Voluntary actions are a subclass of a very much wider genus. Agency is a universal phenomenon. No doubt human agency is what interests us most, but it is absurd to restrict the concept of agency to the actions of human beings. Many of the same verbs of action which we use of humans can be used of animals also: 'eat', 'hug', 'fight', 'pull', 'build', 'migrate', and a host of others. Not only animals, but other living beings are agents—for instance, the grass pushing its way between the crazy paving, the Venus's fly-trap closing on its prey. Agency extends even beyond the realm of living beings: the action of acqua regia on gold, or of hydrochloric acid on litmus paper are genuine actions, not just things that happen to these substances.

In the case of inanimate agents it may take scientific knowledge to identify agency and to demarcate the exact agent; no doubt in the early days of science thinkers were wrong to regard fire and rust as agents. But because some inanimate agents have been wrongly identified in the past it would be absurd to conclude that there are no such things as inanimate agents.

Wherever we can talk of substances in nature, wherever we can talk of natural kinds, we can talk also of natural agency. The concepts of natural substance and natural agency are closely connected with the concept of natural power. The natural actions of an agent are those which it performs in the exercise of its natural powers.

The distinction between the behaviour of humans and the

behaviour of inanimate substances is wrongly demarcated by the theory that only humans exhibit agency. The distinction should be marked as a difference between two kinds of agency, voluntary and natural. However, between the natural agency of non-living things and the intentional action of human beings, there is a hierarchy of agency extending upwards from stones through plants and animals to men.

Living things, unlike non-living natural agents, have needs. Plants need a particular kind of soil if they are to thrive, flowers need water if they are not to die. When we speak of non-living things having needs—as when we say that the fields need rain, or my car needs a new clutch—this is always by derivation from the needs of living beings. The fields need the rain so that the crops can grow, the car needs a clutch so that I can drive it efficiently. The needs are those of the crops rather than the field, of the driver rather than the car. The needs of plants, by contrast, are genuine needs of the plants themselves. But though plants have needs, they do not have wants.

Animals, like plants, have needs, but animals, unlike plants, have wants. Why do we attribute wants to animals but not to plants? There seem to be two reasons. If we are to assign wants to an agent, the agent must have available to it a number of different ways of getting what it needs: it must have not just a single characteristic pattern of activity but a repertoire of different possible actions. Not only that, but the agent must also exercise the activities in its need-satisfying repertoire in cases where there is no need. Animals and plants both feed, but only animals play.

This may seem rather a roundabout way to distinguish needs and wants, or rather to say what want adds to need. Surely the essential thing is that wants can be attributed only to conscious beings. Want, we might say, is just felt need. But this is not correct. First of all, want has to be the kind of feeling that leads in general to action. It is conceivable that felt need might be like a felt ache: it might just cause one to hug oneself and lie immobile. Secondly, and more importantly, it is wrong to think that consciousness can be identified as such independently of wanting. What is the case is rather that the notions of consciousness and wanting become applicable together when the behaviour of an agency manifests the appropriate degree of complexity.

In studying the activity of a complex living organism we are interested in its repertoire of behaviour, its acquisition of information, and its characteristic goals. That is to say, we are interested in its powers, its consciousness, and its desires. If we observe the behaviour of an animal and have knowledge of any two of these factors, we can often infer the third. Given knowledge of an animal's capacities and of the information available to it, we infer its goals from its behaviour: we know which foods dogs like by watching which foods they take from among those they can sense which are within their reach. If we want to study animals' sensory powers, we set them a task within their known capacities (e.g. pressing a bar) which, if they discriminate successfully between different sensible objects, will lead to one of their known goals (e.g. food): from capacity and goal we infer to cognitive information. If we want to test their ability to perform tasks, we provide them with information about means to their known goals: we show them the bananas on the tree and a pair of sticks and see what they can do.

In general, you cannot infer what an animal wants from what it does unless you also know how much it knows and what it is capable of; nor can you infer from its behaviour its state of knowledge or belief unless you know its wants and its repertoire of action. Given a hypothesis about an animal's goals, you can always reject it no matter what its behaviour by attributing to it a particularly bizarre system of beliefs. Given a hypothesis about an animal's beliefs, you can always reject it no matter what its behaviour by attributing to it a particularly perverse set of goals. We avoid methodological breakdown here by making the assumption that the animal's goals centre on the satisfaction of its needs. Since needs can be identified independently of belief or desire there is no circularity in this procedure.

Humans and non-human animals both have wants as well as needs. But just as there is a difference between the needs of plants and the wants of animals, so there is a difference between the kinds of wants which animals have and the kinds of wants which humans have. There are, of course, many wants which are shared by humans and non-human animals: wants such as hunger, thirst, sleepiness, and the desire for sex.

Some languages have a special word for the kind of desire which is common to humans and animals: in classical Greek philosophers called it *'epithumia'* and in medieval Latin the scholastics called it *'concupiscentia'*. There is no natural English way of marking the distinction between animal wants and specifically human wants. But I shall use 'desire' as an English equivalent for *'epithumia'* to mark the animal desires; I shall use 'volition', by contrast, to mark the kind of wanting which is possible only for a language-user like a human being. Both desire and volition, in my terminology, are wants; I shall use 'want' as the word for the genus of which desire and volition are species.

An important difference between desire and volition is that desire, unlike volition, seeks immediate satisfaction: that is, it is a want for something now, a want that is felt more or less continuously until it is satisfied. Volition, by contrast, may be for something distant in time, and may be operative without being an item in the flow of consciousness.

In the case of adult human beings, even the desires of the kinds we share with animals are coloured and modified by our possession of language. For instance, as my hunger becomes progressively more uncomfortable I keep thinking 'still an hour and twenty minutes to go before dinner', using concepts that are well beyond the competence of a hungry dog.

Because of this, for much of our human affective experience there is a degree of artificial regimentation in drawing a line between desire and volition. The nearest we can come in our own experience to pure desire is the case of inarticulate striving to a particular goal from which deviations can be sensed. When I am learning to ride a bicycle, I constantly react by appropriate or inappropriate bodily activity to the tugs and jolts that show I am losing my balance. I do this without being able to give any description in language of the movements with which I strive to recover equilibrium. This kind of experience is a human approximation to pure desire in the case of animals.

When we attribute wants to agents we use various forms of indirect speech; we say, for instance, that Jack wants Jill to come back home, or that the skier wants the children to get off the piste. These constructions may be said to embed what would be the expression, in direct speech, of the want in question: 'Jill, do come back home!' 'Children, get off the piste'.

This feature of language is fully intelligible when we are attributing wants to language-users who could themselves use the forms of direct speech which our indirect speech constructions impute to them. But how can we use the same forms of *oratio obliqua* when we attribute wants to animals, saying, for instance, that the dog wants his master to open the door for him?

It would be foolish anthropomorphism to think that behind the furry brow some doggy equivalent of words is being silently uttered. When we say that a dog wants his master to open the door, we do not need to believe that the animal possesses our concepts of 'master', 'door', 'open', and so on; we need only mean that the dog has a repertoire of concepts, one of which picks out the object we pick out by our concept 'master', another of which picks out the object we pick out by our concept 'door'; and yet another picks out the action we pick out by 'open'.

There is nothing anthropomorphic in the attribution of concepts to animals. But the concepts we attribute to animals must be concepts whose possession can be manifested by non-verbal behaviour. What is anthropomorphic is to attribute to non-language-users concepts whose expression requires the possession of a symbolic apparatus. If an animal has no language, we cannot attribute to it concepts of numbers, or of logical constants, or of abstractions like space, time, and necessity.

The difference between desire and volition is that volition involves the exercise of concepts which need language for their expression, whereas desire need involve only the exercise of simpler and more rudimentary concepts, which can be manifested in non-linguistic behaviour. The kind of behaviour which manifests desire is voluntary action; the kind of behaviour which paradigmatically manifests volition is intentional action.

In some discussions of free will it is implied by philosophers that animals are incapable of voluntary action. But this is a mistake. If voluntary actions are defined as actions which are performed because the agent *wants* to perform them (and not, say, because the agent is pushed or forced), then when animals act to fulfil their desires they act voluntarily. My dog leaps into the river not because I push him but because the pursuit of swimming ducks is his darling passion. If voluntary actions are defined as actions which are performed in circumstances where the agent *can* do otherwise, then when animals choose between

alternatives they act voluntarily. When I call him, my dog can
come home if he wants to; but if he wants rather more to follow
up that interesting smell leading to the cowshed, he can do that
too.

The difference between animals and humans is not that only
humans can perform voluntary actions. It is rather that while
many kinds of animals can perform voluntary actions, only
language-using animals can perform intentional actions or act
for reasons. As we ascend the hierarchy of agency, we rise from
natural agency, through living agency, through voluntary
agency, to the summit of intentional agency.

The claim that dumb animals are incapable of intentional
agency must be further explained if it is not to be misunderstood
and rejected as obviously false. There is no doubt that animals
do things in order to do other things—the cat may scratch at the
door to get into the house, the pigeon puncture the bottle top to
get at the milk. We may ask: is not doing A in order to do B
precisely what intentional action is?

In fact, there is more to the intentionality of action than
merely doing one thing for the sake of another. To show this it is
sufficient to observe that even non-conscious agents, such as
plants and the organs of animals, act in order to bring about
beneficial states of affairs. The roots of plants grow hairs in
order to collect moisture; but neither roots nor root-hairs have
intentions about moisture gathering. It is a function of your
kidneys to separate solid wastes from your blood; but your
kidneys do not have the intention of doing this.

But there is a difference here between plants and animals.
Animals not only act for the sake of goals, they may also be
conscious of their goals, in the quite literal sense that they may
see or smell whatever it is they are after. So why not attribute
intentions to them? It is true that animals do not have the long-
term or remote and universal goals that human beings may
pursue, such as the discovery of scientific truth or the pursuit of
riches. But even if the goals of which animals are conscious are
limited and immediate goals, why should this mean that they
cannot act intentionally?

The grounds for denying intentions to animals rest on the
connection between intentionality and reasoning. When a
human being does X in order to do Y, the achieving of X is his

reason for doing X. But when an animal does X in order to do Y, he does not do X for a reason, even though he is aiming at a goal in doing so. Why not? Because an animal, lacking a language, cannot give a reason for his action.

Does this mean that an agent only acts for a reason if he gives a reason? No. It is possible on a given occasion to act for a reason without giving to oneself or to others any account of the reason. But it is only beings who have the general capacity to give reasons who have the ability to act for reasons. Humans are rational, reason-giving, animals. Dumb animals are not reason-giving animals and therefore cannot act for reasons. The capacity for intentional action is the same thing as the capacity to act for reasons. It is because they lack the capacity to act for reasons that non-human animals lack the capacity for intentional action.

Intentional action presupposes language in the same way as self-consciousness presupposes language. Animals, lacking language, may yet have simple thoughts; Fido may think that there is a bone buried beneath the bush. But unless Fido has a language he cannot have that thought *that he is thinking that* there is a bone buried beneath the bush. For there is nothing in his behavioural repertoire to express the difference between the two thoughts 'There is a bone buried beneath the bush' and 'I am thinking that there is a bone buried beneath the bush'. Similarly, Fido may scratch to get at the bone, and his scratching manifests his desire to get at the bone; but there is nothing within his repertoire to express that *he is scratching because* he wants to get at the bone.

With humans it is different. When my wallet is stolen and I run after the thief, my wanting to catch the thief may be exhibited by my running. Quite independently of that I can express that I am running *because I want to catch the thief*; for I can reply to questions about why I am running, or why I ran. This two-tiered possibility of expression is not open to animals who lack language.

All this is not meant to deny that animals may be conscious of their goals—to quote an earlier example, the scrabbling Fido may well smell the buried bone. But animals are not conscious of their goals *as goals*. Though Fido's conduct shows that the gnawing of bones and sleeping in the chimney corner are among his goals, there is nothing in his behaviour to exhibit the possession of a common concept under which both these ends fall.

What humans have and what animals lack is the ability to perform acts *as answering to a certain linguistic description*. The bank-robber shouts 'put up your hands' and the cashier does so immediately. There may be no hesitation or deliberation; yet the action is a rational one and its rationality depends on the understanding of the words of the command. A dog, to be sure, can learn to obey the commands 'sit' and 'stay'; but the canine reaction differs to even the most instinctive and immediate human one because it is not a response to an element in an articulate system of language. The dog's obedience is not action in accordance with volition.

A volition, in the case of human beings, is a state of mind which is defined by the linguistic description of the action or state of affairs which would fulfil it. There are many different kinds of volition, which can be reported by many different verbs and verbal expressions. 'John wanted Mary to come home' 'Alexander wished for more worlds to conquer' 'Prince Rupert intended to turn the enemy's flank' 'Macbeth felt remorse for having killed Duncan': all these sentences report different kinds of volition. In all cases the object of volition displays a complexity which derives from the complexity of the state of affairs which would constitute its fulfilment: Mary's coming home, Rupert's turning the enemy's flank, and so on. Even when all I want is to get out of here the object of my want is complex: it is that *I* should get out of here.

The complexity of the object of volition is the kind of complexity which we encounter in the distinction between subject and predicate (or, as philosophers would say, argument and function) in a sentence. There is a precisely similar complexity in the objects of belief. The belief that the world is flat has an object which has the same complexity as the wish that the world were flat. We report beliefs in indirect speech, but any report of a belief can be reported also in direct speech: we can say 'James believes this: "the world is flat" '. Similarly, the volitions which we report in indirect speech could be reported in direct speech: 'James wishes this: "would that the world were flat" '. God's knowledge that there is light can be reported by saying 'God knows this: "there is light" '. God's initial command that there should be light can be reported 'God commanded this: "let there be light" '.

The relationship between our voluntary actions and our volitions is, formally speaking, the same as that between actions and commands. By acting we carry out, or fulfil, our own volitions just as by acting we carry out, or fulfil, the commands we are given by others. The relation between a command and its fulfilment, and the relation between an intention and its execution, are both internal, logical relations. That is to say, the description of the content of the command is the same description as the description of the action which obeys it; the description of the content of an intention is the same description as the description of the action which executes it.

For this reason, it is illuminating to take the relationship between command and obedience as the paradigm for understanding the nature of volitions in general. Many different speech acts, and many different mental states, have in common that their appropriate form of expression has the features of the imperative mood. The imperative mood, in its natural uses, is not of course restricted to any single type of speech act: it is used in requests, prayers, advice, instructions as well as in commands and orders. Similarly, mental acts and states such as deciding, intending, wishing, and regretting can all be thought of as states whose expression involves the imperative mood. And all those mental states whose expression involves the imperative mood can be referred to by the term 'volition'.

'Volition' is of course an artificial term, and the grouping of these various specific mental states into a single genus involves a degree of philosophical regimentation. But this is not something without parallel. On the contrary, it corresponds exactly to the way in which philosophers extend the usage of the ordinary word 'belief' to cover the mental counterparts of stating, claiming, conjecturing, opining, admitting, and a host of other speech acts which make use of the indicative mood.

As has already been said, a volition is a *state*. It is a mental state of being favourably disposed to actions, or states of affairs, answering to a particular linguistic description. Volition is not, as such, an action. To have the volition that the train will not be late there is no need for me to rehearse to myself, even in the privacy of the imagination, the words 'Let the train not be late'. It is quite sufficient that it should be the case that if the train is late I will be most annoyed.

Humans, we said, are unlike animals in that they can perform actions as answering to a particular linguistic description. The same point is made when, with the artificial terminology we have just explained, we say that humans, unlike other animals, act in accordance with volitions. But of course the difference between humans and other animals is not exhausted by this. Even spontaneous and unreasoned human action may be in accordance with a volition. If humans are rational animals they must have another capability too: the ability to act for reasons.

To have reasons for action it is necessary, though not sufficient, to have the ability to recognize actions as falling under linguistic descriptions. If someone shouts 'get out of the way' I may do so spontaneously though on reflection I realize that (unlike a cashier in a bank hold-up) I have no reason to do so. To have reasons for acting one must be able to give reasons for acting. Giving reasons for action may take the form of showing the goodness (or putative goodness) of the act itself, or showing that it was a means to some good (or putatively good) end.

To act for a reason it is not necessary that one should actually rehearse the reason, even in momentary silent soliloquy. There are countless cases where one acts for reasons and yet acts immediately without deliberation or reflection. For instance, a physician examining me says 'take a deep breath' and I do so; or, seeing a child running in front of the car, I swerve to avoid it. If these actions are done for a reason then there will be a pattern of reasoning which can be exhibited after the event ('I obeyed the doctor because. . .' 'I turned the steering wheel to the right because. . .'). But the reasons which would appear in the later formulation need not have formulated themselves in the agent's consciousness at the time in order to have been his genuine reasons.

This is not a matter which is peculiar to practical reasoning; something similar is true of theoretical reasoning. We often draw conclusions from a set of premises without formulating any of the premises verbally. Seeing the coat hanging up in the cloakroom we say 'Oh, so John's home' without rehearsing, even in imagination under our breath, the *modus ponens* 'If John's coat is in the cloakroom, John is at home. But John's coat is in the cloakroom. *Ergo*. . .'

There are both similarities and differences between practical and theoretical reasoning. In both the practical and theoretical case we pass from premisses to conclusions, using words like 'therefore' or 'so' to mark the passage from premisses to conclusion. In real life, most practical reasoning, like most theoretical reasoning, is enunciated elliptically in a manner which does not make clear the logical structures involved: as, for instance, in the reasoning 'Winter is coming, and Charles' overcoat is now too small, so I'll buy him a new one'. If this reasoning were to be set out in a logically perspicuous way many tacit premisses would have to be made explicit, such as 'Charles is to be kept warm' 'Charles will not be kept warm if Charles does not have an overcoat' and so on.

One important difference between theoretical and practical reasoning is that a piece of practical reasoning must contain a premiss that sets out a goal to be achieved (such as 'Charles is to be kept warm'). The other premisses commonly set out facts about the present situation, plus information about ways of reaching the goal from that situation. Indeed the commonest pattern of practical reasoning is this: 'G is to be brought about. But if I do B then G. So I'll do B'—where 'G' sets out the goal to be achieved and 'B' describes some behaviour in my power.

This simple pattern is already enough to show that there are important formal differences between the logic of practical reasoning and the logic of theoretical reasoning. For in theoretical reasoning the argument form 'Q. If P then Q. Therefore P' is not a legitimate pattern of deduction, but a well-known form of fallacy.

The difference between the rules of practical reasoning and the rules of theoretical reasoning is connected with a difference between the indicative and the imperative mood. The rules of theoretical reasoning are designed to ensure that we do not pass from true premisses to a false conclusion. They are truth-preserving rules. But the initial premiss and the final conclusion of a piece of practical reasoning are not assertions, true or false. They are rather such things as resolves ('Charles is to be kept warm') and expressions of intention ('I'll buy him a new coat') which belong with the imperative rather than the assertoric mood. What, then, in the case of such reasoning, is the practical analogue of truth, the value which the rules of reasoning seek to transmit from premiss to conclusion?

Practical reasoning is the reasoning we use in planning how to achieve our goals. If there are rules of practical logic, their function will be to see that we do not pass from a plan which is adequate to achieve our goals to one which is inadequate to achieve them. Commonly, in discussing plans, we presuppose our ability to implement them, and try to work out which, of the various plans we might implement, is most satisfactory—which will best serve our purposes and achieve our goals. It is essential in pursuing this kind of discussion that we should have logical rules which preserve satisfactoriness, that in practical reasoning we do not pass from a plan which is satisfactory for a particular purpose to a plan which is unsatisfactory for that purpose. So in the sense in which rules of theoretical reasoning are truth-preserving, we can say that the rules of practical logic are satisfactoriness-preserving.

Though we can speak of different rules for practical and theoretical reasoning, it is perhaps misleading to speak as if there were a practical logic different from theoretical logic. If by a logic we mean a set of logical truths, then one and the same logic is exploited in both theoretical and practical reasoning. It is the patterns of inference which are used to exploit these logical truths which differ. And this is because of the difference between the indicative mood which is the expression of belief in a theoretical truth and the imperative mood which is the expression of the pursuit of a practical good.

It is much more difficult to give an adequate formal account of practical reasoning than to give one for theoretical reasoning. This is because satisfactoriness, unlike truth, is a relative notion. An assertion is either true or false; but a plan is not just satisfactory or unsatisfactory. It may be satisfactory to some persons and not to others, satisfactory for some purposes and not for others.

This means that practical reasoning, unlike theoretical reasoning is—to use a convenient term borrowed by philosophers from lawyers— *defeasible*. In theoretical deductive reasoning, the addition of a new premiss cannot invalidate a previously valid inference. If a conclusion follows from a given set of premisses it can be drawn equally well from any larger set which contains those premisses. With practical reasoning it is not so. A conclusion which would be reasonable from a limited set of premisses may cease to be reasonable from a larger set (mentioning further goals, or extra relevant circumstances). The defeasibility of practical reasoning is something which it is very important to grasp if we are to understand the nature of the will as the faculty for practical reasoning.

In the hierarchy of agents, we have distinguished natural agents, living agents, voluntary agents, and intentional agents. Though agents at each level of the scale have their characteristic types of agency, it would be wrong to think that those at upper levels are capable only of actions of their characteristic type. Human agents, though they are unique in being intentional agents, have the capacity also for the other kinds of agency.

Indeed, human intentional actions appear to be a subclass of conscious voluntary actions. Not all actions of human beings are conscious: snoring, for instance, is commonly not conscious. Not all conscious human actions are voluntary: reflex actions such as blinking under stimulation are conscious but involuntary. Conscious actions are voluntary to the extent that they are under our control. Not all voluntary actions are intentional. For instance, there are the actions which one does not do on purpose, but which can be inhibited with an effort: actions such as wincing in pain, sneezing, fidgeting, laughing, brooding over an injury. Intentional actions are actions which are chosen either as ends in themselves or as means to some other ends: if the actions are chosen for their own sake, then not only are they intentional but they may be called purposes. Intentional actions will commonly bring about unintended consequences and side-effects. The bringing about of such effects constitutes another class of voluntary actions, distinct from the purposeless but inhibitable actions such as yawning and brooding.

If an action is to be voluntary at all, then it must be in some sense done because it is wanted; but if it is to be unintentional it must be wanted neither for its own sake nor as a means to some further end. The sense of 'want' in which all voluntary actions are wanted is a minimal sense. To say that an agent wants, in this sense, to do an action is to say no more than that it is in his power to refrain from doing it if only he will give up one of his chosen purposes. In such cases it is perhaps misleading to say that the agent wants to do the voluntary action in question; more accurately, his doing the voluntary action is the result of his overall volitional state. The important volition is not any purpose to do this action, but some other purpose for which doing this is the price he must (perhaps unhappily) pay. The wanting in question is the wanting of willingness or consent; and consent is something which may be accompanied with varying degrees of enthusiasm diminishing to reluctance and nausea.

We may recapitulate the distinctions which we have made and illustrate them with concrete examples.The word 'want' may cover many types of things, of which it is worth while to distinguish four classes.

First, there are sensual appetites such as hunger, thirst, sleepiness, and sexual attraction: the desires which we have in common with animals. Such desires are mental phenomena in that they are sensations present in consciousness.

Second, there are purposes: wants for long-term and short-term goals which are valued for their own sakes. Such purposes need not be present to one's imagination whenever they are operative. An intention to become an engineer once one's university course is completed may influence one's actions without being an item of consciousness in the way that a headache or a tune hummed in the head may be. By 'purpose' we mean a person's goal in a course of action. We may contrast the purposes which a man pursues with the means he chooses for achieving his goals, and the consequences of his actions which, though he may accept them, are no part of the task he sets himself to achieve. Purpose, so understood, is a particular kind of intention: the ultimate intention of a particular course of action. The unintended consequences or side-effects of the achievement of one's purposes are voluntary.

Third, there are intentions to adopt means to one's ends. These wants, like purposes, may be operative in one's conduct without occupying a place in one's stream of thought; unlike purposes they may concern things not wanted or welcome for their own sake, perhaps even things whose prospect arouses considerable distaste, such as a visit to the dentist.

Finally, there is the kind of want which is the very minimum that is necessary if an action is to be voluntary: the kind of wanting which we may call 'consent'. Something is wanted in this minimal sense if it is something which the agent chooses neither as a means nor as an end, but which would not take place were it not for the agent's pursuit of one of his purposes. I cross a neighbour's field in order to take a swim in the river; as I walk on my way I do a certain amount of damage to the grass and squash a certain number of minute organisms. Doing so is neither a purpose of mine nor a means to my ends; but I do consent to these things: I prefer to do them than to give up my purposes and the means I have chosen.

All of these different kinds of wants can be invoked to explain an agent's action only when it is in the agent's power to act in a manner other than that which amounts to a fulfilment of the want. This is an essential element in the concept of 'want' and in the procedure of explaining action in terms of wants, whatever form of want is in question, whether purpose or intention, whether volition or desire. This conceptual feature is ignored by some philosophers and psychologists—and indeed by some lawyers—who have attempted to introduce the notion of irresistible impulse.

Is there such a thing as an irresistible impulse? How, it has often been asked, can one tell the difference between an impulse which is irresistible and one which is merely not resisted? The difficulty is not merely an accidental and temporary one which progress in scientific techniques may in due course remove. If someone succumbs, for instance, to the temptation of committing a criminal act there is no way even in principle of deciding whether he is a man of normal strength of will who is giving way to impulses which are stronger than normal, or is a man of unusual weakness of will giving way to normal impulses.

Suppose that a question is for decision in court whether the accused acted under an irresistible impulse. If evidence is given to show that on many other occasions he has indulged in criminal behaviour, this may be taken with equal justice as evidence of chronically imperious impulses, or of chronic unwillingness to exercise self-control. If, on the other hand, evidence is given to show that this is a wholly uncharacteristic lapse in a life of otherwise unblemished rectitude, this in turn may be taken with equal justice as evidence of impulses no stronger than normal, or of a degree of self-control well beyond that of the average man. When the same behavioural evidence can be taken with equal justice as evidence for contrary mental phenomena it is clear that the alleged mental phenomena are metaphysical fictions. In the present case, the notion of the strength of an impulse, considered as something ascertainable in total independence of a man's action on such impulses, is a fictional parameter begotten of conceptual confusion.

If an impulse is supposed to be a kind of want, then there is something self-contradictory in the notion of an irresistible impulse. Wants are attributed to people on the basis of what they do when it is open to them to do otherwise. If someone acts under irresistible pressure, then his act is not a voluntary act, and therefore not an act performed because of want. To speak of irresistible impulse is to allow that an action can be both voluntary (because performed on the basis of a want) and non-voluntary (because performed under irresistible pressure).

It may be argued that however incoherent the terminology of irresistible impulse, it is undoubtedly possible for mental disorder to take away voluntary control. It is indeed perfectly conceivable that actions which are within the voluntary control of normal people may, as a result of mental abnormality, cease to be subject to voluntary control. But if they do cease to be subject to voluntary control, that means that they will be performed no matter how much it is in the agent's interest not to perform them. For to say that an action is subject to voluntary control means that it results from the agent's assessment of the attractiveness of the prospect of the action and its consequences in comparison with the other alternatives open to him. If he persists in performing the action no matter what its consequences and no matter what the other alternatives—as may be the case, say, in extreme addiction—then the action is no longer subject to voluntary control.

In discussing intention, I claimed that a person intends the ends he sets himself and the means he chooses to achieve those ends. Some philosophers give the word 'intention' a wider interpretation, so that a man is taken to intend foreseen, but totally unwanted, consequences of his actions. Outside special contexts it is not natural to speak of someone as intending foreseen consequences of his actions when these are unwanted or when he is merely indifferent to them. I know that whenever I walk along a paved street I am very likely to tread on the boundaries between paving stones: but since I passed the age of Christopher Robin I have hardly ever either intended to step on those boundaries or intended not to step on them. Many people drink too much knowing they will suffer a hangover, and eat too much knowing they will put on weight; but they don't drink *in order to* produce a hangover or eat *with the intention of* putting on weight.

The natural concept of intention is that one intends to do what one does for its own sake, or what one does in order to some further ends. Philosophers such as Jeremy Bentham have commended the view that all foreseen consequences of one's voluntary actions are intentional, whether or not aimed at as ends or means. If such a view is not to be a source of confusion one must go on, as Bentham did, to draw a distinction between direct and oblique intention: oblique intention being mere foresight of consequences, and direct intention being the case where the consequences are not just a foreseen outcome, but something which the agent sets out to achieve as a means or an end, and which constituted at least part of his reason for acting as he did.

Oblique intention is primarily a cognitive state: it concerns what a person knows or believes. Direct intention is primarily a volitional state: it concerns what a man wants, either for its own sake or as a means for something else. Of course, if an action is to be voluntary at all, then it must be an action which was done because the agent in some sense wanted to do it. But it may be voluntary without being (directly) intentional if it is wanted neither for its own sake nor as a means to any further end. The sense of 'want' in which all voluntary actions are wanted is the minimal one elucidated earlier: to say that an agent wants to do X, in this minimal sense, is merely to say that he does X consciously while knowing that it is in his power to refrain from doing X if only he will give up one of his purposes or chosen means.

4
Emotion

In the previous chapter a distinction was drawn between the intellect and the will which corresponded with the distinction between two different uses of language: the use of language to describe, and the use of language to prescribe. Very broadly speaking, the intellect is the locus of belief, the state of mind corresponding to descriptive utterances; the will is the locus of volition, the state of mind corresponding to prescriptive utterances. This broad distinction will be refined in a later chapter. But right from the outset it should be pointed out that there is a third use of language which can claim to be no less important than the uses of language to describe and prescribe. That is the expressive use of language.

The use of language to express can indeed claim to be the most primitive and basic use, the one on which the other uses are built. The child's prelinguistic expression of its needs, wants, and emotions is the primitive stock on to which the parents graft the exotic growth of the language used in the community for description and prescription.

The expressive use of language displays kinship with both the descriptive and the prescriptive use. Descriptive sentences are judged true or false in accordance with their relationship to the reality which they seek to describe. Prescriptive sentences are judged good or bad in accordance with the value or disvalue of the state of affairs which they call to be brought about. Expressive utterances may be evaluated in both dimensions. In the dimension of truth they may be graded as authentic or hypocritical, on the basis of the presence or absence in the subject of the sentiment they purport to express. In the dimension of goodness, they may be graded as appropriate or inappropriate to the circumstances in which they occur.

From one point of view expressions of emotion may seem more complex than expressions of belief or volition; from another point of view they may appear more simple. Emotions seem more complex than beliefs and volitions in that they seem to combine belief with volition. This can easily be illustrated in the case of hope and fear: both hope and fear involve a belief in the likelihood of a future event, and combine it in the one case with a positive, and in the other case with a negative, volitional attitude to the event. Many more complicated emotions can be represented in a similar way as combinations of certain kinds of belief with certain kinds of volition.

In another way, however, expressions of emotion are simpler than expressions of belief or volition. The expression of emotion is a more primitive level of language than the expression of pure belief untinged with volition, or pure volition unrelated to belief. It is far easier to identify natural expressions of emotion than natural expressions of pure belief or sheer volition. For this reason, the emotions provide an appropriate terrain for a close study of the relation between the linguistic and the pre-linguistic features of our psychological life. Most human emotions are shot through with thoughts, often of a highly intellectual character; yet it is in the realm of feeling and emotion that we can see most clearly the continuity between child and adult, the kinship between human and animal.

Emotions such as fear, anger, grief, and shame have two important features. They have characteristic bodily manifestations and they have characteristic objects. Fear, for instance, is manifested bodily in such things as trembling and running away. The object of fear is that which we are afraid of. If I am afraid I should be able to say what I am afraid of, there is no similar requirement that if I am hungry there must be some particular thing I am hungry for. Similarly with other emotions: when we grieve there is something that we grieve over, when we feel shame there is something we are ashamed of, when we are angry we must be angry with someone for something.

Here, as elsewhere, a just philosophical understanding of the emotions has to do battle with an opposed Cartesian error. According to the Cartesian picture an emotion is a purely private mental event which is the object of an immediate and infallible spiritual awareness. Emotion is merely contingently connected with its manifestation in behaviour: one might be certain about one's emotional life, according to Descartes, even

if one was in doubt whether one had a body at all. Emotion is
merely contingently connected with its object: Descartes believed
that one could not be mistaken about the existence of a passion,
while one may go wrong in assigning it a cause.

A philosophical account of the affective life of the mind would
need to make careful distinctions between various categories:
feelings such as joy, moods such as depression, emotions such
as love, attitudes such as admiration, virtues such as courage,
and traits of character such as bashfulness. In the Cartesian
classification of the furniture of our minds, these items are all
alike in being passions of the soul. Considered purely as mental
events passions and sensations do not differ from one another
except in the way in which one sensation differs from another.
All alike are items of consciousness, objects of the same infallible
intuition.

Reflection on the nature of the language which we use to
express emotions shows that the emotions cannot be pure
mental events of the kind that Descartes took them for. Any
word purporting to be the name of something observable only
by introspection, and merely causally connected with publicly
observable phenomena, would have to acquire a meaning by a
purely private and uncheckable performance. But if the names
of the emotions acquire their meaning for us by a ceremony
from which everyone else is excluded, then none of us can have
any idea what anyone else means by the word. Nor can anyone
know what he means by it himself; for to know the meaning of a
word is to know how to use it rightly; and where there can be no
check on how someone uses a word there is no room to talk of
'right' or 'wrong' use.

Some people have thought that words for sensations, such as
'pain', stood for private mental events. This is wrong in the case
of sensations; it is doubly wrong in the case of emotions.
Emotions, unlike pain, have objects: we are afraid *of* things,
angry *with* people, ashamed *that* we have done such and such.

This feature of the emotions, which is sometimes called their
'intentionality', is misunderstood if we think that the relation
between a passion and its object is a contingent one of effect to
cause. Many people are attracted by the idea that the meaning of
the word 'pain' is learnt by picking out a recurring feature of
experience and associating it with the sound of the word. It is

much less plausible to suggest that the meaning of 'fear' is learnt in the same way, when we reflect how very different from each other fears of different objects may be.

One cannot plausibly point to a feature of experience, recognizable by introspection without reference to context, which is common to fear of famine and fear of cockroaches, fear of a biting tongue and fear of the dentist's drill, fear of overpopulation and fear of being overdressed, fear of being thought a parvenu and fear of catching AIDS.

The Cartesian picture of the emotions has been so long part of the climate of Western thought that it retains its hold even on those who explicitly reject it, while to those untrained in philosophy it often appears as the natural and common-sense view. Many people are inclined to believe that sensations and emotions are things which we feel within ourselves, by some inner faculty of perception. This thought is made to seem more natural by a misleading feature of ordinary language.

We use the verb 'to feel' in reports both of emotional states and of perceptions. We feel rage, and we feel lumps in the mattress; we feel pangs of guilt and we feel jabs in our forearms. This makes it natural to think that rage and guilt are things which are perceived by those who experience them, as lumps in the mattress and jabs in the forearm are perceived by those on whom they are inflicted. But it is quite wrong to think that emotions are something which are 'felt' in the sense of being perceived by some inner sense.

The assimilation of emotions to perceptions is not, of course, based solely on the grammatical similarity between 'I feel anger' and 'I feel the shape of the coins in my pocket'. There are genuine enough analogies between feelings of emotion and the objects of the senses. Both have similar kinds of duration: a feeling of anger, like a sound, may last for a longer or shorter time. Jealousy may be a pang that comes and goes suddenly like a flash of light in the darkness; or it may last all day like a bitter aftertaste. Emotions, like the objects of the senses, may vary in intensity: grief, like a banging in the next room, may be faint or unbearable, may absorb more or less of one's attention. There is interlinking between different kinds of emotion, as there are networks of relationships between different objects of the same sense: there can be an emotion that is half-way between fear and curiosity, as there can be a colour that is half way between red and blue. Duration, intensity, and blending are properties shared by feelings of all kinds, whether perceptions, sensations, or emotions.

But the differences between emotions and perceptions are more significant than the similarities. Emotions, unlike perceptions, do not give us information about the external world. We can say 'I know there was a policeman there, because I saw a flash of blue' but not 'I know there was a policeman there, because I felt a wave of hatred'. I may discover that someone is dying by noticing a sudden change in her pattern of breathing; but not by feeling a sudden welling of grief in myself.

This feature, while it distinguishes emotions from perceptions, does not mark a difference between emotion and sensation. Sensations do not give us information about the external world any more than emotions do. However, they can give us information about our own bodies, whereas emotions, in themselves, do not even do that. I may learn that I have cut myself by feeling pain, but not by feeling foolish, though my cutting myself may give rise to both these feelings. Of course, at a moment of deep sorrow I may notice that I am in tears; but it is the tears that tell me something about the sorrow, not the sorrow that tells me something about the tears.

Emotions can, indeed, teach one, indirectly, facts about the state of one's mind. A pang of jealousy may be my first clear indication that I am in love, and it may be through being immoderately amused by a childish joke that I come to realize that I have had too much to drink.

A further difference between emotion and perception is that there are not organs of emotion as there are organs of perception. We see with our eyes, smell with our noses, hear with our ears; there are no parts of our bodies with which we fear or hope or feel jealous or excited. There are, to be sure, sensations which are characteristic of different emotions, and these sensations are frequently localized: the lump in the throat, the flutter in the stomach, the legs turning to water. To say that a sensation is localized in a particular part of the body is not to say that that part of the body is the organ of the sensation in question. We do not see colours in our eyes or smell odours in our noses; nor, if we are hearing genuine sounds, do we hear them in our ears. In general, to sense something *in* a part of one's body is not at all the same as to sense something *with* a part of one's body. Quite the contrary: what is sensed with an organ is never a sensation *in* one's body at all.

An organ of a sense seems to be a part of the body which can be moved at will in characteristic ways which affect the operation of the sense, as one moves one's eyes to look in different directions. In this sense of 'organ' there are no organs of emotion. There is no part of one's body which one can bring to bear in order to fear better, in the way in which one can screw up one's eyes in order to see better. One does not have to get into the best position for feeling remorse, as one may have to seek out the best position for listening to a quartet. No part of one's body needs to be trained and conditioned for cat-hating, as one's palate has to be educated and prepared for wine-tasting.

Emotions, in lacking organs, are distinguished from perceptions of colour, taste, smell, heat, roughness, smoothness, and all else which can be felt with a specific part of one's body. But they are not, in this way, distinguished from internal sensations of pain or tickle or heart-throb. Though I feel pain *in* my tooth it is not *with* my tooth nor with anything else that I feel pain; I may feel my heart beating, but neither my heart nor any other part of my body is an organ of this feeling. My stomach is the seat of my hunger, and the organ of my digestion, but it is not the organ of my hunger.

None the less, emotions differ from sensations. Emotions are not localized as pain, hunger, and thirst are. If I have a painful sensation in my toe, then I feel a pain in my toe; but if I have a craven sensation in my stomach, that does not mean that I feel fear in my stomach. It is impossible to imagine hunger in the throat or thirst in the foot; the emotions are not in the same way linked with parts of the body. We do indeed localize emotions, but in the features of others, not in our own bodies. We say not 'I felt terror in my midriff' or 'I felt shame in my cheeks' but 'I saw the horror in his eyes' and 'you could see delight written on her face'.

In some ways, bodily sensations stand half-way between perceptions and emotions. All feelings have duration; but perceptions and sensations are much more closely tied than

emotions to the time which is the measure of local motion. One
can hear a loud noise just for a second, or feel violent pain only
for a moment, no matter what precedes or follows; one cannot
in the same way feel ardent love, or deep grief, for the space of a
second, no matter what preceded or followed this second.

Bodily sensations resemble emotions and differ from perceptions in being linked with characteristic forms of expression.
Hunger is linked with food-seeking behaviour and thirst with
drink-seeking behaviour; there are no similarly specific forms of
behaviour characteristic of seeing and hearing—unless we think
of looking and listening as forms of behaviour. We do indeed
tell the difference between blind and sighted people, and
between deaf people and those with normal hearing, by
observing differences in their behaviour; but we do so not so
much by noticing one particular pattern of behaviour which
they lack as by noticing a specific inefficiency in their behaviour
generally. In being thus linked with specific forms of behaviour
sensations are closer to emotions than to perceptions.

However, there are here distinctions to be drawn within
the class of emotions. Some emotions such as fear and anger
exhibit themselves both in bodily symptoms and in fairly
easily recognizable behaviour. There does not seem to be a
bodily syndrome of hope similar to that of fear, and pity can
show itself in many more varied ways than anger. Some
emotions—we might call them passions—seem to be quite
close, in this respect, to sensations; other emotions seem to
resemble rather thoughts in their capacity for very poly-
morphous expression.

The most important difference between a sensation and an
emotion is that emotions, unlike sensations, are directed to
objects. It is possible to be hungry without being hungry for
anything in particular, as it is not possible to be ashamed
without being ashamed of anything in particular. It is possible to
be in pain without knowing what is hurting one, as it is not
possible to be delighted without knowing what is delighting
one. It is not in general possible to ascribe a piece of behaviour
or a sensation to a particular emotional state without at the same
time ascribing an object to the emotion. If a man runs past me I
can say nothing about his emotions unless I know whether he is
running away from A or running towards B. No flutterings of
the heart or pantings in the breast could tell me I was in love

without telling me with whom. If I am simply in love with being in love, this calls in question whether I am really in love at all.

If we say that emotions have objects, we must make a distinction between emotions and moods. Emotions are such things as anger, fear, and gratitude. Perhaps, in certain contexts, we can make sense of talk of undirected anger, objectless fear, and a vague and diffuse feeling of gratitude. But such cases can be accommodated only against a background of cases where these emotions take an object. If someone had a feeling which never had an object, and was always pointless, there would be no reason to call it either 'anger', 'fear', or 'gratitude'.

There are moods, however, such as cheerfulness or depression, which are not in a similar way tied to objects. Moods resemble emotions in that they involve feelings—one can feel cheerful or depressed just as one can feel angry or grateful—but they differ from emotions in several ways. Though depression may have an object (I may be depressed because I have let my writing get so far behind schedule), it may be simply a generalized feeling which at best fastens on quite inadequate objects such as the unseasonable drizzle or the need to take the cat to the vet. Not only are moods more loosely tied to objects than emotions are, they also lack the specific behavioural expressions which some emotions have. Cheerfulness or depression may come out in the manner of one's behaviour rather than in the substantial form it takes.

Moods and emotions, like other psychological states, may be manifested or kept to oneself. In denying that they are essentially private states one is not denying the possibility of keeping them secret. One is rather denying the possibility that there might be a race of humans who felt all the emotions that we feel, but never manifested them publicly by word or deed. Only beings who are capable of manifesting a particular emotion are capable of feeling it. In particular those emotions which can be manifested only by the use of language (e.g. remorse for a crime committed long ago, or fear about the distant future) can be experienced only by language-using beings.

We might use this fact to draw a distinction between two principal kinds of emotion.

To the first kind belong those which are expressible non-linguistically. These are the ones which are most naturally called passions—they are the ones related to bodily states like hunger, thirst, lust, sleepiness. Passions which are expressible non-linguistically can, of course, also be expressed linguistically. I have already claimed that there is a basic, expressive, use of language on which description and prescription are built.

To the second kind of emotion belong those which are expressible only linguistically. There are emotions which can only be expressed in language just as there are thoughts which can only be expressed in language. To this class belong, among other things, religious sentiments, such as awe, guilt, faith, and worship. We might, indeed, use the word 'sentiment' to indicate this class of feelings: so that the genus of emotion will be divided into the species of passion and sentiment.

Is it correct to say that sentiments can be expressed only in language? Cannot these emotions be expressed also in *action*? They can indeed motivate action; but there is a difference between behaviour which expresses emotion and action which is motivated by emotion. Taking precautions against danger is action which is motivated by fear; but it does not express fear in the way that trembling and cowering do. In the cases where human actions are motivated by sentiments (e.g. romantic love or patriotism) language is still a necessary part of the background against which these emotions are distinguished from other emotions which might motivate similar behaviour (e.g. lust or bravado).

I have said that one can experience an emotion only if one can manifest it, and in particular that those emotions which can be manifested only by language can be experienced only by language-users. But though one can experience an emotion only if one can manifest it, it does not follow that one does experience an emotion only if one does manifest it. There are indeed some emotions for which the stronger thesis holds: a man cannot be in a violent rage or extreme anguish if his countenance is serene and he talks composedly about indifferent topics.

One of the criteria of intensity for such emotions is that they should be incapable of being concealed; as we talk of overmastering anger and overpowering grief. On the other hand, it is clearly possible to be afraid of something, or in love with someone, without telling anybody about it. Is it also possible to experience these emotions without betraying them *in any way*?

There seems to be a difference here between emotions and other states of mind, such as beliefs. It is quite clearly possible to have a belief and to go to one's grave without telling anyone about it and without doing anything about it. We are constantly noticing odd facts and collecting scraps of information (e.g. that there is a fly walking up the window pane, or that the person at the next table in the restaurant is wearing a maroon skirt) which are too trivial either to affect our behaviour or to be worth passing on. But desires and emotions of an agent seem to be more closely linked to action than beliefs are, even if the particular form of action to which they will lead will depend partly on the concomitant beliefs of the agent. The possibility of a completely unexpressed belief does not, therefore, by itself show the possibility of a completely unexpressed emotion.

We must return to the distinction between emotion as motive and emotion as feeling. For an emotion to function as a motive the person whose emotion it is must do something; otherwise there will be nothing for the emotion-motive to explain. If John is in love with Mary then he must in some way or other conduct his life differently from a man who is not in love with Mary. But there seems no reason to think that what is done in such cases must always be something public; perhaps the only upshot of a man's love for a woman may be that he thinks a lot about her. To be sure, in that case, we shall want some explanation why his love goes no further; but such explanations are frequently to be found—perhaps Mary is already happily married.

In some cases, the manifestation of an emotion is the result of a decision; in other cases, it is the non-manifestation of the emotion which is the result of decision and perhaps effort. Thus, we may have to bring ourselves to the sticking point after long preparation in order to reveal our love or confess our shame; on the other hand, it may call for constantly renewed effort to stop our anger breaking out, perpetual vigilance to prevent our fear becoming obvious.

It is possible, then, for feelings of emotion to be kept to oneself, and in that sense to be private. But it does not follow from the fact that some emotions are private events that all emotions could be private events, any more than it follows from the fact that some men are taller than average that it could be the case that all men are taller than average.

The reason why it is not possible that all emotions should be concealed emotions is that if they were, the meaning of emotion-words could never be learnt. The empiricist picture was that one learned the name of a particular emotion by observing in one's own experience the occurrence of a sample of that emotion. On this view, as has already been pointed out, one would never know that the experience one called by the name of a particular emotion was the same as that which others called by the same name. In fact the names of emotions are learned when adults teach children to replace the natural and primitive expressions of them by exclamations and sentences.

A child runs to his mother, and she says 'Don't be frightened' or he trembles and she asks 'What are you afraid of?' Emotion-words are not taught simply as a replacement of emotional behaviour; for what behaviour is characteristic of a particular emotion depends not only on the nature of the emotion in question but also the object of the emotion. If the child cries, for example, we shall know whether to call this pain-behaviour or emotional behaviour only if we know whether he is crying because, say, he has bumped his head or because he has been left alone. The language of emotion must therefore be taught in connection not only with emotional behaviour, but above all in connection with objects of emotion. It is in connection with fearful objects, pleasant tastes, and annoying circumstances that the child learns the verbal expression of fear, pleasure, and anger.

The concepts of individual emotions typically acquire their content from three different sources: from object, from symptom, and from action. The concept of fear, for instance, is linked to fearful circumstances, to symptoms of fear such as pallor and trembling, and to avoidance action such as flight. The concept of remorse is linked to past wrongdoing (e.g. having killed a friend), to symptoms such as weeping, and to action to palliate the harm done, such as making provision for the family of the dead one. In the standard case, which is the paradigm for learning the nature of a particular emotion, and is the scenario most easily interpreted as the occurrence of emotion, all three factors will be present: as when the man-eating tiger advances roaring and the defenceless planter screams and takes to his heels.

Not all the three elements must be present in every case of bona fide fear. Humans are often afraid of things which are not in themselves at all fearful; they often repress the symptoms of fear; and in the presence of impending danger they may fail to take avoidance action, either because they think flight ignoble or because the fear is so great as to be paralysing. But if there is no danger, no slightest symptom of fear, and no action taken at all, it is difficult to make sense of a person's avowal of fear. No doubt the minimum that is required for a psychological state to deserve the name 'fear' is that it should be a state in which the verbal expression of fear comes naturally to someone who has learnt and customarily exercises the normal use of the word 'fear'.

But the avowal of fear in a sufficiently abnormal context may well remove the intelligibility of the avowal. If a man says he feels frightened, but shows no signs of fear and takes no particular action, we will understand and may believe him; but not if, when asked why, he says 'because it is five to three, and I always feel like this at five to three'. Whatever his feeling is, why does he call it 'fear'? If a man regularly used the word in the way described above, then all that we could say was that he did not understand what it meant; and of any word in an unknown language which was regularly so used, we could say for certain that it did not mean fear.

The concepts of the several emotions are employed not only in the description of feelings but also in the explanation of actions. We feel fear, and we also act out of fear; love is not only a sentiment, but also a motive of action. It is tempting to think that to say a person acted out of a certain emotion is to say that his action was preceded and caused by the occurrence of the corresponding feeling. But this is incorrect. The relation between feeling and motive is a more complicated one.

To exhibit the relationship we must begin by comparing motive with intention, a concept with which it is clearly connected. Roughly speaking, when a reason for action concerns something prior to, or contemporaneous with, the action, it is a motive; when it refers to some future state of affairs to be brought about by the action, then it expresses an intention. 'Why did he kill him? Because he had killed his father'—there we have a motive, revenge. 'Why did he flatter the Prime Minister? In order to become a bishop'—there we have an intention. As these examples illustrate, the distinction between motive and intention is hardly a sharp one.

The notion of intention is much more basic than that of motive. Long passages of narrative can be written without reference to motives, while no narrative of human behaviour will make sense if it is devoid of reference to intentions and intentional actions. It is possible to act from a motive without having any concept of that motive; it is not possible to act for an intention without possessing the concepts expressed in the intention.

Motives, we have said, are backward-looking reasons for action. But there are many such reasons which are not the kind which spring to mind when we talk of motives. 'I'm coming indoors because it's too cold out here' 'They sacked him because he turned up drunk three days running' 'He bought a new suit because the old one was too small'. These sentences obviously have something in common with 'I killed him because he killed my father'. Yet there is no motive-word which occurs naturally in connection with the first three sentences as 'revenge' does with the fourth.

Each sentence exemplifies a common pattern of description and explanation of human conduct. First, there exists a state of affairs which the agent dislikes; then the agent does something; then there exists a different state of affairs which he likes better. This pattern has numerous simple exemplifications: I am cold, I go to the fire, and I get warm; I am dirty, I wash myself, and I become clean.

Wherever this scheme is appropriate there will be room for three main types of explanation of action. An action may be explained by reference to the unwanted state of affairs which preceded it, or by reference to the wanted state of affairs which was, or was expected to be, its upshot, or by some form of explanation which alludes to both of these together. If we are to understand someone's action we want to know how she is better off (or thinks she is) or the world is a better place (or is thought to be) as a result of the action. This can be explained by reference to the badness of the preceding state of affairs, or by reference to the goodness of the (expected) succeeding state of affairs. Or the action may be classified as one of a well-known type productive of some specific form of amelioration.

The important distinction is between forward- and backward-looking reasons for action. Reports of intentions give forward-looking reasons for action; reports of motives may either give a backward-looking reason, or exhibit the action as falling under some specific scheme of this general pattern. Which backward-looking reasons we will naturally call 'motives' depends on the comparatively trivial circumstance of whether or not we have a name for the specific scheme exemplified. Where we have a common type of undesirability in the pre-action state of affairs, or a common type of desirability in the post-action state of affairs, we assign names to the particular pattern of action, and speak of action out of—for instance—fear, jealousy, or ambition.

Intentions can often be deduced from motives, and vice versa; for a report of an intention fills in in detail part of a pattern which a report of a motive sketches out in general. The reason why one can act from a motive without having the concept of it is that one's action may correspond to a particular pattern without one having named the pattern in question.

Because a motive is a kind of reason, however, the agent must be aware of the particular features which make the relevant pattern applicable. I cannot act out of revenge if I do not know that the person I am setting out to injure has done me any harm. If in certain circumstances we can attribute unconscious motives to agents, we must simultaneously attribute to them awareness, at some level of consciousness or unconsciousness, of the relevant features. If my attitude to a friend is to be explained as the result of unconscious jealousy, there must be some level of awareness at which I believe that he is enjoying some benefit which should more appropriately belong to me.

Moods are much less linked to motives than emotions are. If I dawdle on my way to work because I am depressed, my depression may cause my dawdling but it does not provide a motive for it. Because causes, unlike motives, are not reasons, there is nothing untoward in the idea that a mood may affect my action without my noticing the mood. Similarly, whereas if one feels an emotion one must be aware of its object, there is no reason why one should not undergo a mood without being aware of its cause. A woman may not realize that her depression is the result of pre-menstrual tension; she may well not have noticed how many weeks have passed since her last period.

Many names of motives are names of virtues and vices, because the patterns of action which it most interests us to single out and name are those by which we judge the goodness or badness of an agent. Thus, actions intended to bring about forms of good to particular classes of people in particular circumstances may be described as performed out of pity, gratitude, or a sense of justice.

Few, if any, actions bring about only the result desired by an agent. The other results brought about may be states of affairs which the agent does not want, or which are bad for him, or which are injurious or displeasing to others. Frequently there will be names of motives to apply to these patterns also. A soldier who runs away through fear may bring it about not only that he is no longer in danger, but also that he is no longer in a position to carry out his orders; and so his action exemplifies the pattern not only of fear but also of cowardice. It is thus that the names of vices come to be used in the attribution of motives to human agents.

To act out of a certain motive, I said earlier, is not to act in consequence of the occurrence of the corresponding feeling. It would be nearer the truth to say that on the contrary a feeling is a feeling of a certain emotion only if it occurs in the context of an action fulfilling a certain motive-pattern. But this is an exaggeration: feelings are linked more directly to the symptons of an emotion than to motivated action. (The distinction between the two can be illustrated once again in the case of fear: trembling is a symptom of fear, avoidance behaviour is motivated by fear.) Actions, to be motivated, must be voluntary; symptoms are not producible at will even where they can be checked at will. The symptoms of fear, or anger, or grief, where they occur, do not greatly differ no matter what is feared, or gives rise to anger, or causes grief. Behaviour motivated by these emotions differs systematically in accordance with the object: behaviour actuated by fear of getting fat differs from behaviour actuated by fear of getting thin.

Feelings of emotion are the sensations linked with the symptoms of an emotion; but the sensations are emotional feelings, just as the bodily changes are emotional symptoms, only if they occur in a certain context. The context which attaches the sensations and the bodily changes to a particular emotion is itself specified as an emotional context by its relation to the pattern of action characteristic of the emotion in question. Going pale, for instance, is a symptom of fear only if it occurs in the face of at least putative danger; and danger is itself a backward-looking reason for actions which are motivated by fear. Thus feeling is linked to symptom, symptom to object, and object to action. The verbal expression of fear, in its turn, is linked to symptom, circumstance, and action; and once established becomes itself a new criterion for the feeling.

In attempting to give an account of how the concepts of the emotions interlock with other concepts I have concentrated on cases where the linguistic expression of emotion is embedded in the kind of context where emotion could be attributed even to non-language-users. In the terminology introduced earlier, I have analysed the concept of emotion by taking the passions as the paradigm for explication. But of course all but the simplest emotions in human beings cannot be given adequate expression by a mere avowal of passion. One emotion differs from another, in human beings, above all by the thoughts in which the emotion is articulated. The course of love, for instance, cannot be portrayed without a description of the thoughts of the lovers. The higher emotions which we have called sentiments are individuated, as thoughts are, by the forms of language which give them expression.

Though our treatment of the emotions has concentrated on the elemental passions which animals at least partly share with humans, it has not been for that reason ill-proportioned. For the topic of the sentiments does not need separate treatment in the same way, since the philosophical analysis of sentiments is englobed in the more general question of the nature of thought, to which we will return in Chapters 8 and 9.

5

Abilities, Faculties, Powers, and Dispositions

In discussion hitherto much use has been made of the notion of ability: the intellect, for instance, was defined as the capacity to acquire intellectual abilities. It is time to turn philosophical attention on to the notion of *ability* itself. An ability may be thought of as a particular kind of possibility or power: the nature of ability may be investigated by studying some features of the English word 'can' and its equivalences in other languages.

The first philosopher systematically to study the different types of possibility was Aristotle. He drew distinctions between various kinds of potentiality and power which were later systematized by scholastic philosophers in the Middle Ages. Active powers (e.g. the power to heat) differed from passive powers (e.g. the power to be heated). Natural powers (such as water's capacity to wet) were to be distinguished from rational powers (such as a pharmacist's ability to prescribe). Natural powers needed certain preconditions for their exercise: fire will burn wood only if the wood is sufficiently dry. But if these conditions are met, then the power will infallibly be exercised. The case is not the same with rational powers. A pharmacist may have the skill to prescribe, and may have the necessary pharmacopoeia; but he may fail to prescribe if his patient does not have sufficient funds. Natural powers, unlike rational powers, are also *tendencies* to act in a certain manner.

The possession of rational powers, according to Aristotle, is peculiar to human beings. Among the powers of humans there are some which are innate—the senses, for instance—while others, like the ability to play the flute, are acquired by practice. The liberal arts, and in general the skills which are the fruits of education, are powers of a particular kind. Not only are they *abilities* whose exercises are the relevant scientific, artistic, and craft activities; but they are themselves *actualizations* of the capacity to learn which is presupposed by education. They can thus be called actualizations as well as potentialities.

Medieval philosophers introduced a technical terminology here: the skills were first or primary actualizations in contrast to the episodic employment of the skills which were secondary actualizations. Thus the ability to speak Greek is a first actualization, while the actual utterance of a Greek statement or command, or the understanding of a particular Greek text on hearing it, is a secondary actualization.

These distinctions in the Aristotelian tradition were made in the context of the discussion of the Greek and Latin words which express the relevant concepts. The English auxiliary 'can' is used in a wide variety of contexts which go far beyond the realm of active and passive powers as discussed by Aristotle.

First, there is the 'can' of logical or formal or mathematical possibility, as in 'nine can be divided by three' and 'equals can be substituted for equals'. Then there is a different use of 'can' in such sentences as 'the mild winter could be the result of the depletion of the ozone layer' or 'The Prime Minister could have authorized the leak herself'. When we say, in this sense, that something can or could be the case, we mean that it is consistent with the available evidence that it is or was the case. This kind of possibility is called by philosophers 'epistemic possibility'.

These two senses of 'can', in this context, need to be mentioned only to be set aside. Neither logical nor epistemic possibility is relevant to the notion of ability which is central when we are studying the human abilities which are the subject matter of the philosophy of mind. Within the narrower area which interests us we may distinguish four senses of 'can'. There are four different types of thing we may be attributing when we say of someone or something that he or it *can* do such and such.

First, there are natural powers such as the power of fire to burn and of water to freeze. As Aristotle observed, when the conditions are right for the exercise of a natural power, the power will inevitably be exercised: necessary conditions here are also sufficient conditions. A philosopher who is attracted by determinism is likely to consider this type of power as the paradigm, to which he will attempt to reduce all other types.

Second, there are abilities, such as a dog's ability to run or retrieve and a human being's ability to swim, paint, or do long division. These differ from natural powers: no matter how propitious the external conditions, an agent may on occasion refrain from exercising an ability because he does not wish to exercise it. (Abilities of this kind overlap with, but do not coincide with, Aristotle's category of 'rational powers'.)

Third, there are opportunities for the exercise of abilities. I may have the ability to swim, but in another sense of 'can' I cannot swim if there is no water around. I may have the ability to read, but no opportunity to do so if I am stranded on a desert island with seven gramophone records but no books.

Fourth, there is the overall sense of 'can' in which it indicates the presence of both ability and opportunity. This is the kind of power which is in question when the issue of free will is discussed. Libertarians are accustomed to define freedom as being the power to do otherwise. In order to do X freely , it may be said, one must have the power to do other than X; that is, one must have both the ability and the opportunity not to do X.

Philosophical problems in the philosophy of mind often arise from confusions between different senses of 'can'. Both ability and opportunity are sometimes confused with epistemic possibility, that is to say, with the 'can' of consistency with known data, where 'it can be that p' means 'it may be that p' or 'p, for all we know to the contrary'. But for our concerns the most important distinction is that between ability and opportunity.

An ability is something internal to an agent and an opportunity is something external. Opportunities are circumstances which permit the exercises of abilities. If I am to have an opportunity to do something there must be no external impediment to my doing it. Impediments to doing things may be internal as well as external: I cannot speak French when I am asleep, and I cannot play rugby if I have a broken leg.

Neither internal nor external impediments to the exercise of abilities take away the abilities themselves: there remains an important difference between the sleeping French speaker and the sleeping monoglot Briton, and between the invalided rugby international and the complete novice to the game. Internal impediments perhaps may be said to diminish or suspend abilities rather than to take them away. External impediments remove opportunities, but internal impediments do not do so, even though they suspend abilities. However, in suspending the abilities they remove temporarily the possibility of taking the opportunities.

Suppose now that there exists no external impediment to the exercise of an ability, and no internal impediment similar to sleep or injury; and suppose that the possessor of the ability fails to exercise it because he does not want to exercise it. Does his lack of volition, or volition to do the opposite, remove either the ability or the opportunity to perform the relevant action? The answer to this question is clearly crucial to an understanding of the freewill problem.

It is clear that choosing not to exercise an ability does not in itself remove the ability. Having made my choice, I may change my mind only a few moments later and prove, by exercising the ability, that I still possess it.

There are, of course, some abilities which if not exercised may weaken and eventually vanish. If, having once left school, I never again make use of my hard-won ability to recite by heart *The Charge of the Light Brigade*, then when in old age I wish to do so I may find I have forgotten the poem and lost the ability. But not all abilities are like this: after several decades of abstention I may still find myself able to swim or to ride a bicycle.

In no case of ability does a single decision to abstain from exercise remove the ability. Abilities, unlike opportunities, are inherently general: there are no genuine abilities which are abilities to do things only on one occasion. This is true even of abilities, such as the ability to kill oneself, which of their nature can never be exercised more than once. Even if no more than one opportunity arises for the exercise of an ability it must always be conceivable that it should have been exercised on some occasion other than the one on which it is in fact exercised.

Nor does choosing not to do something remove the opportunity for doing it; for as we have said, opportunities, unlike abilities, are external to an agent. If the only thing which stops you from doing something is the fact that you don't want to do it, you cannot say that you had no opportunity to do it. I am away from home for three weeks and I fail to write to my wife: when I return home I cannot avoid her reproaches by saying 'I had no opportunity to write: whenever I had a spare moment I was prevented by a strong contrary desire to go to the singles bar'.

Nor does the lack of a volition to exercise an ability, or the presence of a volition to do something else instead, suspend the ability in the way that sleep or injury may do. Indeed, paradoxically, the volition not to exercise an ability can itself be regarded as a different kind of exercise of that ability. Aristotle thought that it was characteristic of the powers of rational agents that they were two-way powers, powers which could be exercised or not at will. To the extent that this is true, when I choose not to exercise an ability I am manifesting that ability no less than when I choose to exercise it. That is, only someone who possesses the ability to speak French can choose, on a particular occasion, not to speak it. If I am in Paris without knowing a word of French, then my silence and my incomprehension are not matters of choice.

Volitional powers are powers which I can exercise if I choose. But it is important to be clear about the sense of 'I can if I choose'. Many philosophers have thought that in the expression 'I can if I choose' the 'if' clause expresses a condition on the ability. (Very varied views have been held about the nature of the condition.) But it is a mistake to read 'I can if I choose' as equivalent to 'if I choose, I can'. 'I can if I choose' is elliptical for 'I can do X if I choose', where the context will indicate the appropriate substitution for X; and the 'if' clause is to be taken with 'do X', as 'do-X-if-I-choose'.

The reference to choice here qualifies the exercise, not the ability. The ability to weep is an ability which I have and which a new-born baby does not have. But the ability to weep-when-I-choose is not something I have, though I might acquire it if I went to drama school.

The Aristotelian distinction between natural and logical powers is related to the distinction between natural and voluntary causes. A natural cause, according to Aristotle, is 'determined to one thing'. That is to say, in the order of nature, if the causal conditions in a situation can be fully specified, a single effect can be infallibly predicted. In the order of voluntary behaviour, it is not so: when a man does something, for instance, because he is asked to, his doing it cannot be predicted infallibly even by someone who knows everything that has been said by him and to him throughout his life up to the request itself.

This distinction, of course, does not solve, but merely sharpens, the problem of free will. Natural effects can be predicted from natural causes, voluntary effects cannot be predicted from voluntary causes. Just so: but voluntary actions are also natural events, and the interesting and difficult question is whether voluntary effects can be predicted from natural causes.

Let us look more closely at the nature of ability itself. Abilities are distinct from their exercises: an ability is a more or less enduring state, the exercise of an ability will be a datable event or process. Consider the ability of paracetamol to relieve pain. The possession of the ability is clearly distinct from its exercise: the pills possess the ability while they are bottled up in the medicine cabinet, but only begin to exercise it after being swallowed.

Abilities must be distinguished not only from their exercises but also from their possessors and their vehicles.

Abilities, like other dispositions, are qualities or properties: but what are they qualities of? What is the subject in which they inhere, the possessor to which they belong? It seems obvious enough that a man's beliefs and virtues are *his* beliefs and virtues. All attributes are in the last analysis attributes of substances: all a man's dispositions are dispositions of a human being; what believes, or is generous, or is healthy is, strictly speaking, a man, and not his mind or his heart or his body. So too with abilities: the possessor of an ability is what *has* the ability: I am myself the possessor of my abilities such as the ability to ride a bicycle or the ability to use language.

The possessor of an ability must be distinguished from other capacities or abilities which may be hierarchically related to the ability in question. It is I, and not my mind, or my language-faculty, who know English and am exercising this ability in writing this paragraph. Still, there are conceptual relationships between different abilities, and it is not senseless to ask such questions as whether skill in writing history is principally a gift of memory or imagination. To ask which faculty is exercised through a certain disposition or manifested in a certain type of action is to seek for the conceptual connections between abilities of various kinds.

The vehicle of an ability is the physical ingredient or structure in virtue of which the possessor of an ability possesses the ability and is able to exercise it.

The distinction between abilities and their vehicles is not something which is peculiar to human beings and their abilities. Vodka has the power to intoxicate: the vehicle of the power of vodka to intoxicate is the alcohol the vodka contains. Similarly, my car has the ability to decelerate: it can go slower in answer to the touch of my foot on the brake. The vehicle of this ability is the brake mechanism.

A vehicle is something concrete, something which can be weighed and measured. An ability, on the other hand, has neither length nor breadth nor location. This does not mean that an ability is something ghostly: my front-door key's ability to open my front door is not a concrete object, but it is not a spirit either.

In discussing abilities, and indeed dispositions and attributes of all kinds, the philosopher must be constantly on his guard against the temptation to hypostatize them, that is to say, to treat them as if they were substances or parts or ingredients of substances. A power or capacity must not be thought of as a thing in its own right, for instance as a flimsy actuality or an incorporeal vehicle. The difference between a power and its exercise or vehicle is a category difference, not a difference like that between solid and shadow.

This is a point which is true of dispositions in general, and not just of abilities. In one of Andersen's fairy-tales the goblin takes the housewife's gift of the gab and gives it to the water-butt. To think of a disposition as a piece of property which may be passed from owner to owner is one way of hypostatizing it. Another way, by contrast, is to think of a particular disposition as the kind of thing somebody might have two of, to ask questions such as how many senses of humour Oliver Cromwell had. A third way is to treat the relationship between a disposition and its exercise as a contingent and not a logical matter, as if it were a relation of cause and effect similar to that between smoking and cancer.

The presence of virtue in a man does not account for his

virtuous actions in the way in which the presence of alcohol in a drink accounts for its intoxicating effects; for the presence of alcohol, unlike the presence of virtue, can be ascertained by methods other than the observation of the effects to be explained. This was what was forgotten by the physicians who explained that opium put people to sleep because it had dormitive power. The statement was philosophically correct; but the physician's job was to look for the vehicle of the power rather than hypostatizing the power itself. Hypostatizations of dispositions in this way are futile because any disposition is defined by its exercise and individuated by its possessor.

The distinction between abilities and their vehicles is not restricted in its application to the abilities of human beings, as our examples have illustrated. But the distinction has many applications in human affairs and it must be kept clearly in view if we are to avoid confusion in thinking about the nature of the mind. The senses, for instance, are powers of human beings; the organs of the senses are the vehicles, or part of the vehicles, of the sense-faculties. Thus, my eye is part of the vehicle of my ability to see, and my ear is part of the vehicle of my ability to hear. Parts of my brain are also parts of the vehicle; but neither the eyes, the ears, nor the relevant parts of the cortex can be identified with the faculties of sight and hearing.

An important instance of the distinction between possessor, ability, and vehicle is the distinction between people, their minds, and their brains. Human beings are living bodies of a certain kind, with various abilities. The mind, as we have said, is the capacity to acquire or possess intellectual abilities. The vehicle of the human mind is, very likely, the human brain. Human beings and their brains are physical objects; their minds are not, because they are capacities. Once again, to say that the mind is not a physical object is not to say that it is a ghostly spirit. If I insist that a mind is not a physical object with a length and breadth and location, that is not out of devotion to spiritualism, but simply out of concern for conceptual clarity.

The distinctions which I have been making are not novel: they are, as I have said, developments of distinctions which go back at least as far as Aristotle. However, in every age philosophers have been tempted to blur the distinctions. In philosophy there is a perennial temptation to reduce potentialities to actualities.

Some philosophers attempt to reduce powers to their exercises: thus, explicitly, David Hume, who said the distinction between a power and its exercise was frivolous. Some philosophers attempt to reduce powers to their vehicles: thus, implicitly, Descartes, who wanted to identify the powers of bodies with their geometrical properties.

Philosophical errors about capacities in general show up particularly vividly when they occur in the philosophy of mind. Applied in this area, exercise-reductionism becomes behaviourism: the attempt to identify mind with behaviour consists in treating the complex second-order capacity which is the mind as if it were identical with its particular exercises in behaviour. Applied in this area, vehicle-reductionism becomes materialism: the attempt to identify mind with brain consists in reducing my mental capacities to the parts and structures of my body in virtue of which I possess those capacities.

Materialism is a grosser philosophical error than behaviourism because the connection between a capacity and its exercise is in truth a more intimate one than the connection between a capacity and its vehicle. In the case of the mind, the connection between capacity and exercise is a conceptual connection: one could not understand what the mind was if one did not understand what kinds of thing constitute the exercise of mental capacity. The connection between capacity and vehicle, on the other hand, is a contingent one, discoverable by empirical science. Aristotle's grasp of the nature of mind will stand comparison with that of any subsequent philosopher; but he had a wildly erroneous idea of the relationship of the mind with the brain, which he believed to be an instrument to cool the blood.

If the mind is not a physical substance, how can one talk, even metaphorically, about the mind having parts, such as the intellect and the will? Can the mind have a structure at all, if it is not a concrete object? The answer is yes, provided that we are clear what kind of structure we are talking about.

The set of abilities through which the mental capacity is exercised have relationships to each other, and these relationships between abilities form the structure of the mind. There are, for instance, relationships between the ability to multiply numbers and the ability to take square roots. This is not something peculiar to minds, and the structure in question is not a ghostly partitioning. Not only human beings have abilities which are structured in this way: we can discover the structure latent in the operations of a pocket calculator by identifying the algorithms it uses (which we might do, for instance, by identifying the different kind of rounding errors which occur in its output).

There is a distinction between the structure of the mind, in this sense, and the structure of the brain which is its vehicle. Here again, the analogy with the calculator helps to make the point clear, because there too there are different kinds of structure: it is the mathematician who identifies the structure of the algorithm, the engineer who is the expert on the structure of the electronic hardware.

If we anatomize the mind into faculties, the major articulation which the philosophical tradition presents us with is the distinction between intellect and will. What is the basis of this distinction, and what exactly are we doing when we inventory faculties in this way? And once we have distinguished between intellect and will, what can we say about the relationship between them?

Human beings do many things such as understanding, judging, feeling, desiring, deciding, intending. Philosophers ascribe these different states and activities to different faculties. Why do they do this? What is it to ascribe particular actions to one or other faculty? It is to group the actions together in virtue of common features of description and assessment which apply to them.

Among the characterizations we may assign to human mental states and actions, there are two which stand out as specially important. We may characterize certain states as true (or false); we may characterize others as good (or evil). Beliefs, most obviously, may be described as true or false; desires, most obviously, may be described as good or evil. Those states and activities which can be evaluated on the true/false scale belong to the cognitive side of the soul; those states and activities which are evaluated on the good/evil scale belong to the affective, volitional side of the soul. At the highest level, the truth-bearing (or falseness-bearing) items are actualizations of the intellect; the goodness-bearing (or badness-bearing) items are actualizations of the will.

States of the will and activities of the intellect may both be described as right or wrong. It is wrong to think that the earth is larger than the sun, and wrong to have vengeful strategies. However, the wrongness in the one case consists in falsehood, and in the other case in evil. The wrong, we might say, adopting a tone of archaic grandeur, is the genus of which the false and the bad are species. Similarly, the human mind is a capacity of which the primary faculties are the intellect (which thinks truth or falsehood) and the will (which pursues good or evil).

Both intellect and will can be thought of as faculties whose activity is to assent. Given a description in language of a possible state of affairs, we may assent to it as a description of what is the case, or as a description of what is to be made the case. In each instance we can assent to it by saying 'yes'; but in the one case by saying 'yes' we affirm a proposition as true; in the other case by saying 'yes' we accept a proposal as good. In each case, our assent may be evaluated as right or wrong. But there is a difference between the two cases: a difference which philosophers have characterized by the phrase *onus of match*.

Whether we assent to a proposition or a proposal, we are assenting to a description of a possible state of affairs. But let us suppose that the possible state of affairs does not, at the relevant time, obtain. Do we fault the assent or the state of affairs? Do we condemn the original assent as a false assertion, or do we complain about the subsequent state of affairs as an unsatisfactory outcome? The different answers which can be given to these questions bring out what is meant by saying that the onus of match between the description and the state of affairs is different in the two cases.

Consider the different relation which a building has to an architect's plan, and to a plan in a guidebook. Suppose there is a difference between the building and the plan. If the plan is in a guidebook, it is the plan which is wrong; if the plan was made by an architect, there is a mistake in the building. So, in general, in assenting to a proposition (a statement), we place an onus on a piece of language to match the world; in assenting to a proposal (a command or project) we place an onus on something non-linguistic (primarily, our own actions) to match a piece of language. Our assents to proposals may be judged good or bad; but they are not judged bad (as an assent to a proposition is judged false) simply because they do not match what eventually happens in the real world.

The distinction between the intellect and the will corresponds to a distinction between two modes of speech, the indicative and the imperative. When we speak in the indicative mood the facts, or what happens, set the standard by which the utterance is measured: the utterance is judged either favourably as true or unfavourably as false. In the imperative mood (interpreted broadly as in Chapter 3) the utterance sets the standard by which the facts, or what happens, are measured: what happens is judged either favourably as good, or unfavourably as bad.

There used to be a philosophical slogan: truth and falsity are in the mind, good and evil are in things.

Truth and falsity are in the mind: that is, it is statements and beliefs that are true and false, and whether a statement or belief is true or false depends on what the facts are; the facts are the standard by which statements and beliefs are judged. Here, something in the world sets the standard by which something in the mind is judged.

Good and evil are in things: that is, it is things, and states of affairs, that are good or bad, and the standard by which they are judged good and bad is set by commands and volitions concerning them. Thus, whether an agent makes a mistake in what he does depends on what his intentions are. Whether a servant's actions are obedient or disobedient depends on what her mistress's commands are. Whether a citizen's acts are legal or illegal depends on what the laws are. Whether a particular state of affairs is good or bad depends on what somebody wants or might want. In all these cases, something in the mind—in the broadest sense — sets the standard by which something in the world is judged.

The distinction between the two great faculties of intellect and will, then, rests on the distinction between two different relations which thoughts or states of mind may bear to the reality which is their topic. And thoughts can bear these two different relations to reality because the utterances which express them bear the same two different relations to reality.

The linguistic facts which we have been considering cast light on the distinction between intellect and will. But they show also that the mental anatomy which consists of intellect and will is excessively simple, and may obscure the real nature of the abilities which are clustered together when we talk of faculties.

In contrasting indicative and imperative utterances, we have laboured the fact that there is a distinction between the prediction or judgement that the Democrats will win the next election and the wish or hope that the Democrats will win the next election. But beside the differences there is also something in common between the two states of mind. That is to say, the state of affairs which would verify the prediction is the same as the state of affairs which would consitute the fulfilment of the wish. The state of affairs in each case is: the Democrats winning the next election.

Whether to make the judgement or to have the wish, a person must understand the sense of the sentence 'The Democrats will win the next election'. To understand the sense of that sentence is not the same thing as to assert its truth. For the understanding of the sense of the sentence remains the same whether the sentence appears as a complete communication or as a clause in a longer sentence. When the sentence occurs as a clause, as in 'If the Republicans do not reduce the deficit, the Democrats will win the next election', it retains its sense, but it is not asserted as it is when it appears on its own.

We could bring out what is in common between the judgement and the corresponding wish by rewriting the expressions in the following artificial manner:

> The Democrats winning the next election: true!
> The Democrats winning the next election: good!

The part of each of these expressions preceding the colon indicates the state of affairs which is the topic both of the judgement and of the wish. The part after the colon corresponds to the different mood of the different states of mind and their expression: in the first case, the prediction that the description of the state of affairs will come true; in the second case, the conviction that the state of affairs described is a good state of affairs.

By setting out in this artificial manner the way in which the judgement and the wish both resemble and differ from each other we can see why the distinction between intellect and will is not altogether satisfactory. For we have not two but three abilities involved here. There is first the ability to understand the sense of the sentences, to know what the Democrats winning the next election amounts to. Then there are the two distinct abilities to judge the sentence as true or to express the sentence as a wish. Traditional talk of the intellect often confounds together the ability to understand with the ability to judge. If we are to talk of faculties it is better to talk of three faculties: the faculty of judgement, the will or faculty of volition, and the intellect or faculty of understanding which is exercised both in judgement and in volition.

The intellect will then be the faculty by which we grasp the meaning of the words and sentences which we use in judging and in willing. As such, it will be considered at length in a later chapter. But two points need to be made now about the relationship between meaning and judging, since these two functions are amalgamated in the traditional account of the intellect.

First, there are cases where it is impossible to understand the meaning of a sentence without judging it to be true. This is the case of self-evident statements—obvious analytic truths. In the general case, any thought which has the complexity of a sentence may be a true thought—a thought that is in accord with the facts—without being judged to be true. But in the case of self-evident truths, failure to assent to the truth of the relevant proposition would be taken as a sign of having failed to understand it.

In many philosophical systems the assent to self-evident propositions has been regarded as one of the most significant of all human intellectual activities, and sometimes 'the intellect' is used in the narrow sense for the ability—indeed the infallible propensity—to assent to such truths. Other philosophers have thought that in these cases the very fact that understanding is alleged to bring assent in its train shows that no true judgement is involved. I do not wish here to take sides in this argument, but merely to give notice that I will not use intellect in this narrow sense, but will continue with the distinction just made between the intellect and the faculty of judgement.

Secondly, when we say that the intellect is the faculty concerned with meaning, we have to distinguish between two different senses of 'meaning'. There are two different ways in which human beings confer significance on what they say: first of all, they use words and sentences with a certain meaning; and secondly, they may or may not mean what they say. Whether an utterance is meant seriously is quite a different question from what is the sense of the utterance. The words and sentences in a play have the same sense as they would have if uttered in real life; but the actors in uttering do not mean them seriously as they would if they uttered them outside the context of the play. The question 'did you mean that seriously?' can rise about commands as well as about statements, or indeed even about mere suppositions. And the question is not a question about one's understanding, but about one's intentions. It is an enquiry, not into the state of one's intellect, but into the state of one's will.

Indeed, the distinction between the faculty of judgement and the faculty of volition can be brought out in a new way by reference to this concept of *meaning* and utterance. There are different criteria of sincerity for different kinds of utterance. An assertion or statement of a sentence is insincere if the sentence is not *believed*. The utterance of a command, or the expression of an intention, is insincere if it is not *meant*. The difference between the two criteria of sincerity shows the difference between those utterances which express acts and states of the faculty of judgement, and those which express acts and states of the faculty of volition.

There is another difficulty in assigning the intellect and the will as the two great faculties of mind. The two do not seem to be faculties in the same way. The will does not seem to be, as the intellect is, a cluster of abilities which can be exercised in action. We may try to bring out the contrast in three different ways.

If we say that the will is a faculty it seems that what we are saying is that a being has a will if it has the power to intend, choose, decide, enjoy, regret, and so on. But if these are the characteristic exercises of the will, then it seems that the will is not a set of capacities in the way in which the intellect is a set of capacities. To possess intelligence is to possess, *inter alia*, the capacity to learn how to do sums; but there is no performance which stands to the faculty of the will in the relationship which the performance of doing sums stands to the faculty of the intellect. For intending, choosing, deciding, enjoying, regretting are not activities in the way in which doing arithmetic, and even learning to do arithmetic, are activities.

We may give an intelligible, and in certain contexts adequate, account of a person's activity by saying 'she is doing arithmetic'.

We cannot similarly report an activity by saying 'she is intending, she is choosing, she is deciding, she is enjoying, she is regretting'. For intention and regret appear to be states rather than activities, and if we are to know what she is doing in the other cases, with the same degree of adequacy as when we know she is doing arithmetic, we need to know what she is choosing, what she is deciding, and what she is enjoying.

Again, we can test and measure the intelligence of different human beings by observing their proficiency in suitably selected tasks. Such testing, no doubt, involves a degree of tightening up, and possibly tendentious redefinition, of the everyday concept of 'intelligence'; but the concept produced by this exercise is a perfectly comprehensible one and is useful for many of the same purposes as the everyday concept is. But it seems that no amount of rigorization of the concept of 'will' would put us in a position to allot candidates volitional quotients as we can allot them IQs. We can, of course, test and measure such things as the perseverance of candidates in particular tests. But in testing such things we are not testing candidates' wills in the way in which we are testing their intelligence in getting them to spot the odd man out in a series. For the abandonment of an attempt to solve a problem is just as much a voluntary action as the continuance of the attempt; whereas the failure to spot the odd man out is not just as much an intelligent performance as the successful spotting.

Intellect and will both seem to be capacities at some remove from action—this is part of what is meant by calling them 'faculties' rather than simply 'abilities'. But the way in which they are remote, or second-order, abilities does not seem to be the same in the two cases. The intellect is a second-order ability in that it is an ability to acquire abilities. If we are to regard the will as a faculty, it seems that we must regard the ability of which it consists as being a second-order ability in a different sense: as the ability to do things in a certain way, namely voluntarily or intentionally.

These three difficulties do not show that there is no faculty of will. What they really show is that there is more than one faculty of will: that is to say, that those who have spoken of the human will have had two different aspects of human abilities in mind. These we must now distinguish.

In our previous discussion we have introduced the will as essentially the capacity for having language-formulated wants. The will, understood in this sense, is a faculty precisely parallel to the intellect as the capacity for having language-formulated beliefs. The intellect and the will, so understood, can be thought of as two facets of the capacity for the mastery of language and the acquisition of all the other abilities which language makes possible. Intellect and will, so understood, are symmetrical, and indeed inseparable. The indicative and imperative uses of language are mastered together; we do not find children who can understand the word 'bread' in statements, but not in commands, or who can master the indicative forms of the verb 'eat' but not the imperative ones.

But those who talk of the will, and especially of the freedom of the will, have in mind something which is not on the face of it at all the same as the ability to have volitions. They have in mind the power to act voluntarily: that is to say, the power to act in accordance with one's wants and in the presence of open alternatives. Let us continue to use the name 'will' for the ability to have volitions; and let us introduce the artificial expression 'the power of liberty' for the power just mentioned. The power of liberty will in its turn have two aspects: the first, traditionally called 'liberty of spontaneity,' is the power to act in accordance with one's wants; the second, traditionally called 'liberty of indifference', is the power to act in one way when one could have acted otherwise. These two aspects of the power of liberty, as I shall later argue, are inseparable from each other.

The power of liberty, on the other hand, does seem to be capable of existing in agents which do not possess wills. The higher animals can act out their wants and choose between alternative courses of action, but they do not have the ability to formulate desire in language. What I have called 'the power of liberty' is called by many philosophers 'free will'. I rejected this name for it, because to use it would involve accepting the seemingly absurd conclusion that animals have the freedom of the will without having any will to be free. But rightly understood there is nothing paradoxical in the idea that animals have free will, in the sense of the power of liberty.

So the power of liberty can exist without the will. Can the will exist without the power of liberty? Some philosophers have thought that God, and holy angels, and human beings enjoying the delights of heaven, had such a clear intellectual vision of what was the best thing to do on each occasion that there was no real possibility of them acting otherwise than for the best. In the case of human beings in the world we know, the will appears to involve the power of liberty. And in fact, this seems to be not a contingent truth about frail humans, but a conceptual necessity.

This can be shown by reflection on the concepts of *act, want,* and *power.* Though not every want is acted on, the power to *have* wants of a certain kind is inseparable from the power to *act on* wants of that kind. Therefore, the power to have volitions is inseparable from the power to act on one's volitions. But a volition is a kind of want, and the power to act on a want is the power to act voluntarily. Therefore, the power to act on one's volitions is the power to act voluntarily. Hence, finally, the power to have volitions is inseparable from the power of liberty.

Having distinguished the power of liberty from the will, one must ask how the power of liberty is itself related to the will and the intellect. To do this, we must look once again at the concept of *disposition* and point out some differences between dispositions of the will and dispositions of the intellect and of the power of judgement.

The notion of *disposition* in its turn is best approached via the notions of *capacity* and *action.* Human beings have many capacities which animals lack: the capacity to learn languages, for instance, and the capacity for generosity. These capacities are realized in action when particular human beings speak particular languages or perform generous actions. But between capacity and action there is an intermediate state possible.

When we say that a man can speak French we mean neither that he is actually speaking French nor that his speaking French is a possibility which might have been realized if he had been brought up in Marseilles. (Still less are we saying that his speaking French is a mere logical possibility.) When we call a man generous we mean more than that he has a capacity for generosity in common with the rest of the human race; but we need not mean that he is doing something generous at the moment of our utterance. It is states such as knowing French and being generous which philosophers have in mind when they speak of 'dispositions'. A disposition, we might say, is half-way between a capacity and an action, between pure potentiality and full actuality.

Knowing French is an intellectual disposition; generosity is a disposition of the will. There is a difference between dispositions of the two kinds. To be generous is *inter alia* to be able when the occasion demands to put others' interests before one's own. To know French is *inter alia* to be able when the occasion demands correctly to conjugate irregular verbs. If, when the occasion demands, one fails to put others' interests before one's own, one fails, *pro tanto*, to be generous. But without detriment to one's knowledge of French one may fail to give an irregular verb the conjugation which the occasion demands—perhaps as a trap to one's pupils. To be generous it is not enough to be able to put others first: it is necessary actually to do so. To know French it is not necessary to write one's French verbs correctly; it is enough to be able to do so.

We may distinguish, within the realms of both intellect and will, between general and specific dispositions. Language skills such as knowledge of French, and virtues such as generosity, are general dispositions. By contrast particular concepts, beliefs, and volitions are particular dispositions. The mastery of a particular concept—the understanding, for example, of the word 'inflation'—is a particular disposition of the intellect. A particular belief, such as the belief that the world is round, is a particular disposition of the power of judgement. A particular volition, such as the intention to give a bunch of flowers on Mother's Day, is a particular disposition of the will.

There appear to be different kinds of relationship between disposition and exercise in all three cases. Possession of a concept seems to be like the possession of a natural power in that wherever the appropriate circumstances present themselves for the understanding of a word such as 'inflation' (e.g. if one meets it in a book one is reading) one cannot help but understand it: necessary conditions for exercising the understanding seem to coincide with sufficient conditions for exercising it. This seems to be true at least of the passive exercise of understanding: it may be, of course, that I refrain from any active use of language which would involve calling upon my understanding of the word 'inflation'.

Neither beliefs nor volitions seem to be like concepts in this respect. But there is a further contrast between dispositions of the will and dispositions of the faculty of judgement. For if beliefs and volitions are both dispositions, only volitions appear to be tendencies. A volition to catch the train will, in the absence of countervailing volitions, amount to a tendency to take steps to catch the train. Beliefs are not tendencies in the same way.

The belief that the earth is round finds expression in saying 'the earth is round'; but it is not a tendency to say this, for even when the occasion arises to say it, one may not wish to do so and yet believe it to be true. Nor, of course, is the belief the mere capacity to say 'the earth is round' which is shared by flat-earthers, provided that they know English. Between capacity and action, therefore, there are two possible intermediate states: dispositions which are tendencies and dispositions which are not.

Beliefs and volitions, though they may both be described as dispositions, and contrasted in this way as something habitual rather than something episodic like a particular action or utterance, should not be thought of as being habits. Dispositions are not the same as habits (though all habits are dispositions). The difference between the two may be brought out crudely thus. If one has a disposition to do X then it is easier to do X than if one has not: examples are being generous and speaking French. If one has a habit of doing X then it is harder not to do X than if one has not: examples are smoking and saying 'I say' before each sentence.

6
Self and Self-Knowledge

WHAT can be more intimate or important to each of us than our self? The poet Thomas Traherne wrote:

> A secret self I had enclos'd within
> That was not bounded with my clothes or skin.

(Poetical Works, London, 1903, p. 49.)

The self of which Traherne speaks is what is most personal and private to each of us. Most people never see beyond our clothes; a few intimates have seen the uncovered nakedness of our skins; but no human being other than myself has seen my self. Other people—each of us may feel—can know me in a sense, but what they can know of me is only what is exterior; however familiar they may be with me, however hard they may try, they can never reach to the real self within.

The philosophical concept of the self has been given dramatic expression by another poet, Arthur Hugh Clough. In a powerful though incomplete verse drama, *The Mystery of the Fall*, Clough identifies the self as the locus of the primeval sin of Adam. He makes Adam claim for his innermost ego nothing less than divine status:

> Though tortured in the crucible I lie,
> Myself my own experiment, yet still
> I, or a something that is I indeed,
> A living, central, and more inmost I
> Within the scales of mere exterior me's
> I—seem eternal, O thou God, as Thou.

(*Poems*, OUP, Oxford, 1974, p.169.)

Clough was an extraordinarily introspective person, with a morbid fear of the slightest insincerity or affectation. It is no accident that he should be able to express so vividly the thought that one's public selves are a carapace to be sloughed off.

It is significant, however, that he places this thought in the mouth of the sinful Adam. Other writers have seen the self as the locus not of sin but of sanctity. Robert Bolt, in his play *A Man for All Seasons*, makes the motivating force which takes Thomas More to martyrdom his hero's 'adamantine sense of self'. More, says Bolt, was a man who knew how far he would yield to love and to fear, but who became rigorous and unyielding when at last 'he was asked to retreat from that final area where he located himself'. More died rather than swear a false oath, because, as he says in the play, 'When a man takes an oath he's holding his own self in his own hands. Like water; and if he opens his fingers then, he needn't hope to find himself again.'

But of course it is not poets and dramatists, but philosophers who are most given to talking about the self. The *Oxford English Dictionary* lists a special philosophical sense of the word 'self' which it defines as follows:

That which in a person is really and intrinsically *he* (in contradistinction to what is adventitious); the ego (often identified with the soul or mind as opposed to the body); a permanent subject of successive and varying states of consciousness.

It is the purpose of this chapter to claim that the self of the philosophers is a mythical entity, and so likewise is the self of the poets and dramatists to the extent to which it is modelled on the philosophers' myth.

At one level, 'the self' is a piece of philosopher's nonsense consisting in a misunderstanding of the reflexive pronoun. To ask what kind of substance my *self* is is like asking what the characteristic of *ownness* is which my own property has in addition to being mine. When, outside philosophy, I talk about myself, I am simply talking about the human being, Anthony Kenny; and my self is nothing other than myself. It is a philosophical muddle to allow the space which differentiates 'my self' from 'myself' to generate the illusion of a mysterious metaphysical entity distinct from, but obscurely linked to, the human being who is talking to you.

The grammatical error which is the essence of the theory of the self is in a manner obvious when it is pointed out. But it is an error which is by no means easy to correct; that is to say, it is by no means easy to give an accurate account of the logic, or deep grammar, of the words 'I' and 'myself'.

It will not do, for instance, to say simply that 'I' is the word each of us uses to refer to himself, a pronoun which when it occurs in sentences is synonymous with the name of the utterer of the sentence.

This is not difficult to show. Julius Caesar, in his *Commentaries*, regularly described his own actions in the third person, using the name 'Caesar'. (In our own time General de Gaulle sometimes affected a similar manner of speaking.) There might be a language, call it Caesarian, in which there were no first person pronouns, and in which everyone talked about themselves by using their own names. We may ask whether everything we can say in English can be said in Caesarian. The answer is clearly no. If Caesar wishes to deny that he is Caesar (perhaps wishing to test the perspicacity of a new petitioner at court, like the Dauphin faced with Joan of Arc) then in English he can tell the lie 'I am not Caesar'. In Caesarian no similar option is open to him. 'Caesar is not Caesar' will not do the trick. Nor will 'the person who is speaking to you is not Caesar'. For in Caesarian that sentence in Caesar's mouth is equivalent to the English sentence 'The person who is speaking to you is not I'.

The truth is that 'I' does not refer to the person who utters it in the way in which a proper name refers to its bearer. Neither does 'myself'. This does not mean that these words refer to something else, say my self. In fact, neither 'I' nor 'myself' is a referring expression at all. It is, of course, true that the truth-value of sentences uttered by X containing the words 'I' and 'myself' will be determined by what is the case about X. But this fact about the truth conditions of such sentences does not determine the meaning of the items within the sentence. The grammatical error which conduces to the belief in a self is this false belief that 'I' is a referring expression.

But though belief in a self is in one sense a grammatical error, it is a deep error and one which is not generated by mistaken grammar alone. The error has a number of different roots, and these need to be pulled up if the weed is to be eradicated. I shall concentrate in this chapter on two of the roots: the epistemological root and the psychological root. The myth of the self takes different forms in accordance with the root from which it takes its growth.

The epistemological root of the notion of the self is Cartesian scepticism. In his *Meditations*, Descartes convinces himself that he can doubt whether the world exists, and whether he has a body. He then goes on to argue 'I can doubt whether I have a body; but I cannot doubt whether I exist; for what is this I which is doubting?' The 'I' must refer to something of which his body is no part, and hence to something which is no more than a part of the human being Descartes. The Cartesian ego is a substance whose essence is pure consciousness, the mind or *res cogitans*.

Attempts to give content to the notion of a Cartesian ego run into two insoluble problems. The first problem concerns the relation of that ego to the body from which it has been distinguished. How can an ego, belonging to a spiritual realm, act upon or be acted upon by a material entity? The second problem concerns the relation between the underlying mental substance and its successive conscious states. What right has Descartes to assume that passing thoughts inhere in any substratum at all? Either of these problems is sufficient to prevent any coherent content being given to the notion of *res cogitans*.

The *res cogitans*, it may be thought, is the self in the second of the philosophical senses identified by the *OED*: the ego identified with the soul or mind as opposed to the body. However, we should note that the epistemological route to the notion of the self takes us to a self which is much more circumscribed than the notion of the soul or of the intellectual mind described in this book. For the Cartesian ego is the substratum of those states of mind about which doubt is impossible. But there are many states of mind which are not exempt from doubt and where the first person is in no position of infallible authority.

The mind is the set of faculties whereby I understand, judge, know, believe. It is far from being the case that whenever I think I understand, judge, know, or believe something I do in fact understand, judge, know and believe that thing. If Descartes wishes to say that we are infallible about the contents of our own minds, the most he can claim with plausibility is that we know what we are thinking at a given moment.

No one, Descartes might say to you, is better placed than yourself to answer the question 'A penny for your thoughts?'— and while in answer to that question you may lie you cannot be mistaken. Surely, you may think, I am infallible about what I am visualizing in my mind's eye, or saying to myself in my head! That is something which I *know*, and which *only* I know, or at least only I *really* know, since others will have to take my word for it and they cannot be sure I am not deceiving them.

If Descartes is identifying himself with the contents of his mind in this sense, then what he is identifying himself with is his imagination, not his intellectual mind. The images of inner vision, and the words of inner monologue are what Descartes' scholastic predecessors would have called 'phantasms', exercises of the imaginative fancy rather than of the intellect.

Now of course, the intellect and the imagination are linked: these phantasms have the significance they have because of the intellectual capacity of the imaginer. If I do not know French I cannot talk to myself in French any more than I can talk to you in French. None the less, the procession of imagined French words in the fancy is something quite different from the intellectual ability in which knowledge of French consists.

Among the activities which genuinely belong to the mind is the activity of doubting. Here, surely, one might think, Cartesian infallibility applies. We may be mistaken about what we know or understand, but surely we know when we are doubting! But even this is wrong. Even the words used to give private expression to Cartesian doubt would not have any sense in a world which contained nothing but a Cartesian ego. And this fact gives the death-blow to the whole Cartesian programme.

The Cartesian ego is one version of the myth of the self: the version which grows from an epistemological root. A different and richer version of the myth is to be found in empiricist philosophy after Locke. This grows not from an epistemological root but from a psychological root: it derives from a particular picture of the nature of introspection.

The Lockean self no less than the Cartesian ego takes its rise from a confusion between the intellect and the imagination. However, it owes its particular character to an erroneous picture of the imagination which has been accepted by philosophers in many different traditions, namely the view of the imagination as an inner sense.

As will be shown in a later chapter, the objects of imagination are misdescribed when imagination is conceived as an inner sense. But more seriously, the notion of an inner sense misrepresents also the subject of imagination. The self, as misconceived in the empiricist tradition, is essentially the subject of inner sensation. The self is the eye of inner vision, the ear of inner hearing; or rather, it is the mythical possessor of both inner eye and inner ear and whatever other inner organs of sensation may be phantasized.

Hence, if the whole notion of inner sense is misconceived, then not only the objects of imagination are misrepresented as inner sense-data, but so also, more importantly, there is a misunderstanding underlying the idea that there is an inner subject of sensation, the self of empiricist tradition.

If I am right, the self of modern philosophical theory is a chimera begotten of empiricist error. But, notoriously, thoroughgoing empiricism has recognized that it has a problem in making room for the self. Empiricism teaches that nothing is real except what can be discovered by the senses, whether inner or outer. The self, as inner subject, can clearly not be discovered by the outer senses, which perceive only the visible, audible, tangible exterior of things. But it cannot be discovered by the inner sense either.

It is well known that Hume, after the most diligent investigation, failed to locate the self.

When I enter most intimately into what I call *myself*, I always stumble on some particular perception or other, of heat or cold, light or shade, love or hatred, pain or pleasure. I never catch *myself* at any time without a perception, and never can observe anything but the perception. . . . If any one upon serious and unprejudic'd reflexion, thinks he has a different notion of *himself* I must confess I can reason no longer with him. All I can allow him is, that he may be in the right as well as I, and that we are essentially different in this particular. He may, perhaps, perceive something simple and continu'd, which he calls *himself*; tho' I am certain there is no such principle in me.

(*Treatise of Human Nature*, Oxford, 1896, p 252.)

Herbert Spencer stated clearly the reason why this failure to discover the self was not merely a contingent matter, not something to be attributed to the Scottish philosopher's inattentiveness or sloth. Self is, by definition, the inner perceiver; therefore it cannot be anything that is inwardly perceived: 'If, then, the object perceived is self, what is the subject that perceives? Or if it is the true self which thinks, what other self can it be that is thought of?' (*First Principles*, London, 1875, p. 65). For empiricism, the self is an unobjectifiable subject, just as the eye is an invisible organ. But just as the Cartesian ego dwindles to nothingness when Cartesian scepticism is rigorously applied, so too the empiricist self vanishes when subjected to systematic empiricist scrutiny. The self is not discoverable by any sense, whether inner or outer; and therefore it is to be rejected as a metaphysical monster.

Very intelligent and sophisticated philosophers of our own age, who are well aware of the internal inconsistencies of Cartesian rationalism and British empiricism, none the less accept the notion of the self, as something different from the human being whose self it is. The self, it may be suggested, is essentially a perspectiveless subject of experiences. Ordinary persons, that is to say, see the world from a particular viewpoint; the objective self takes the view from nowhere. An objective self does indeed ordinarily view the world from a certain vantage point, namely the life of the person whose self it is. But this is not the point of view of the true self, because the true self can take an objective view of its owner as merely one item among the contents of the world. Perhaps, indeed, it would be conceivable that there should be a self which was not identical with, or specially linked to, any person of an ordinary kind.

Philosophers who take this view find it difficult to make precise what is the relationship between a person and his or her self. In some contexts they are likely to say that people *have* selves; in other contexts that they *are* selves. In either case it is clear that a self is not to be in any straightforward way identified with a tangible body of flesh and blood.

Philosophers who believe in selves, when they write books, use the first person pronoun, just as other authors do. But the reader of such philosophers must ask himself who or what it is that is indicated by the word 'I' which occurs from time to time in sentences in their writings. The normal conventions would entitle the reader to assume that the utterer of these 'I' sentences is the author whose name appears on the title-page. However, the sentences themselves often speak as if the author of the book—the writer of flesh and blood—were something different, if not distinct, from their utterer—something that the utterer makes use of, and is acquainted with. We know, however, that the voice or hand which transmitted these thoughts to paper was the voice or hand of the author; so we are left with the eerie feeling that the author is being used as a medium, or ventriloquist's doll, by a spiritual, objective entity speaking through him. We others, of course, can never be directly acquainted with the author's self; we have to take the author's word for his self's existence, or at best we have to accept the author as speaking to us on his self's behalf.

What leads a philosopher to claim that he has a self which is something different from himself, something that he *is* over and above being an ordinary human being, something that he *has* over and above having a mind and a body? There seem to be two main motives. The first is a desire to make sense of the sentence 'I am N.N.' in the context of soliloquy. The sense of 'I' must be different from the sense of 'N.N.' if the sentence is not to be empty. The second is a feeling that there is something incongruous in a person's having the thought that he is an insignificant item in the vast oceans of space and time. Since I cannot help seeing the world from my own viewpoint, the conception of a centreless universe in which I am just a tiny speck must belong to something other than me.

Neither of these considerations is persuasive. There are many contexts in which the utterance of 'I am Anthony Kenny' has a clear sense: a self-introduction at a cocktail party; the expression of recovery from amnesia after bad concussion; the realization, by a schoolmaster named John Smith, that it is he whom the schoolchildren have been referring to by the nickname 'Anthony Kenny'. But the utterance of 'I am Anthony Kenny' which is supposed to support the existence of the objective self is not anything like this. It is supposed to be an identity sentence consisting of two referring expressions with different senses, on the model of 'The morning star is the evening star'. But this is the wrong way to construe sentences of the form 'I am N.N.' whether in public utterance or in private utterance. And there is no reason to believe that every utterance of 'I am N.N.' sentences in private will have any sense at all, any more than an utterance of 'Come here!' to oneself in the middle of a soliloquy.

In the second place, I find it difficult to understand what is problematic about a person's having the thought that he is an insignificant speck in the universe. No doubt this is a matter where each person should speak for himself, but for my part I find no difficulty in believing that Anthony Kenny is a person of no cosmic significance. There were countless ages before I was born, there will be countless ages after I am dead; everything I know is minute compared with all that I do not know, and my hopes and fears are of infinitesimal consequence in the overall scheme of things. To be sure, a great deal of my effort goes into seeking the welfare of this tiny transitory being that is myself; but there is no disproportion here since in the light of eternity my endeavours are just as puny as the purposes they serve.

The point is that in all this it is the human being, Anthony Kenny, who is speaking, and it is the human being, Anthony Kenny, who is being spoken about. What is supposed to be incoherent about such self-reference? Why should either the subject or the object of these thoughts be detached from the everyday human being who is doing the thinking of them?

Shall we say that human beings must see the world from a viewpoint, and therefore a perspectiveless vision must belong to something other than an ordinary person?. If we take the word 'see' literally, then it is true that we can only see from a particular point in space, and that we cannot see the organ of our vision. (It is, I believe, only contingently true that I cannot see the back of my neck; but it is necessarily true that an eye cannot, save in a mirror, see itself.) But if we take 'see' in the broad intellectual sense, to include having beliefs and making judgements about the world, then it does not seem true that we can only see the world from a viewpoint. When we make scientific judgements we are making impersonal, centreless judgements; and the objects of our scientific judgements can perfectly well include ourselves. I can talk about myself, and talk about myself talking about myself; and if I can talk about myself I can think about myself, either aloud or to myself.

The only reason for denying that it is logically possible to think objectively about oneself seems to be a hangover from the empiricist view of the self. If one thinks of solitary thought on the model of the inner sense, then the contents of the mind are images which are presented to an inner eye in the internal theatre of the imagination. And just as the outer eye cannot see itself, so the inner eye cannot see itself. The true self is therefore thought of as an unviewed viewer. But it is only if we first confuse thought with imagination, and then conceive imagination simply as interior sensation, that we have any reason to deny the possibility of thought about oneself. The very same I, the very same human being, the very same Anthony Kenny is both the thinker of this thought that you are reading and the topic of this thought that you are reading.

For the poets whom I took as the point of departure for this chapter, the self had two essential characteristics: first, it was a secret and private entity, and secondly, it was that part of a human being which was most lasting and essential, by comparison with superficial and accidental features. Now it is no part of my thesis to deny that there are elements of our human life that are private, or that there are elements that are fundamental. What is wrong with the doctrine of the self is that it identifies the fundamental with the private.

Much of my life is private in the sense that it consists of thoughts and feelings which I keep to myself and do not express to others. Like most people, I accompany much of what I do with fragmentary inner monologue; each day I have feelings, suffer moods, entertain fantasies which I do not trouble to inform other people about. Because these episodes in my life are not made public, they may seem to be peculiarly mine, very intimate to myself. The philosopher's 'self' was invented partly to be the bearer, or observer, of these secret thoughts and passions. Self-knowledge, according to the philosophy of the self, is the monitoring of this inward life.

It would be absurd, however, to claim that my private imaginings consitute that which, in the words of the *OED*, is really and intrinsically me in contradistinction to what is adventitious. To be sure, someone who had access to all my private imaginings would know a little more about me than someone who was privy only to my public utterances: she would learn, for instance, about various remarks which had come into my mind to make but which I had suppressed for reasons of prudence or politeness. But remarks which occur and are not even made are at least as adventitious items in my life as remarks which are actually made. Indeed, the fact that I suppressed certain remarks is often a more important fact about me than the fact that they came into my mind in the first place.

The really important questions about oneself, about what

kind of person one fundamentally is, are not questions which can be settled by introspection. 'Do I really love her?' 'Am I the kind of person that would betray a friend to death to save my life?' 'Will I regret, in five years time, that I changed my job in mid-life?' 'Am I getting more and more vain as I grow older?' These, and countless other questions of the same kind, are questions which receive their definitive answer not in private colloquy with oneself in the imagination, but in the testing conditions of life in the real and public world. A close friend or spouse may well be able to conjecture in advance with greater perspicacity than I the answers they will eventually receive.

As with self-knowledge, so with self-love. When I am selfish, the good which I am pursuing is the good of the human being, Anthony Kenny; not the good of some inner entity in the theatre of the imagination. Those who pursue pleasure and power for themselves are seeking not pleasure and power in the inner world of the imagination, but in the public world of flesh and blood. Unselfishness, too, is measured not by interior acts of secret renunciation, but by the willingness to put first the interests of other human beings in the public world. The self that is cosseted or disciplined is not the inner observer of the mental theatre, nor the centreless subject of objectivity: it is the human being with all the parts and passions of a man.

7
Sensation and Observation

AMONG the capacities which human beings have and share with other animals are the senses. It has been for centuries traditional to speak of the five senses: sight, hearing, taste, smell, and touch. Philosophers and psychologists have from time to time wished to add to the number five, or to suggest that one or other of the five should be regarded as an amalgam of capacities rather than as a single sense. There may be good reason for this, and there are certainly considerable differences among the canonical five senses themselves. Let us, however, for our purposes, consider the ways in which the five resemble each other and the reasons for grouping them all together as senses.

Each of the senses is a way of acquiring knowledge about the environment, about the properties of items in the world around us. Each of the senses is a discriminatory ability and each of the senses is a capacity for experiencing particular kinds of pleasure and distress. Each of the senses has an organ: that is to say, there is a part of the body, which has a particular sensitivity to the objects of the particular sense, as the ear has to sounds and the eyes have to colour and light.

It should not be thought that every part of the body which is necessary for a particular mode of perception is an organ of perception. Damage to the visual area of the cortex may make a man blind; for all that, the cortex is not an organ of sight as the eye is. What then is an organ of perception? It is a part of the body which can be moved at will in characteristic ways which affect the efficiency of the sense in question. Thus, part of what is involved in the concept of sense-organ is expressed in such remarks as 'You can see it if you look through this crack' 'You can hear them if you put your ear to the wall' 'If you don't like the smell, then hold your nose'.

The most obvious difference within the group of five senses is between those which act at a distance and those which do not.

We can hear noises made far away, and see light coming from immense distances. To touch or taste something one has to have it within reach. The sense of smell can reach beyond the immediate tactile environment but cannot compare with hearing, let alone sight, in its capacity to reach into distance.

The objects of the senses are the phenomena which can be detected by them: thus colours are among the objects of vision, and sounds the object of hearing. In the case of smell and taste the same name is used both for the faculty and for its objects: we smell smells and taste tastes. By touch we discern many different properties of tangible objects, such as shape, softness, smoothness, mass. There are several ways by which we can detect, with our senses, whether things are moving or stationary: we may see the rabbit motionless, hear the train coming, feel the daddy-long-legs crawling up the spine.

Some but not all of the objects of the senses are properties of substances. Among the sensible properties of substances we may distinguish two classes. There are those properties, such as colour and taste, which can be detected only by the operation of a single sense; and there are those properties, such as shape and motion, which can be detected by more than one sense. In ancient and medieval philosophy the first class were called proper sensibles, and the second common sensibles. A very similar distinction was made in more modern philosophy between secondary and primary qualities, to use the terminology introduced by John Locke.

All these are obvious facts about senses which are known without either philosophical reflection or empirical enquiry. Over the centuries philosophers have analysed the concepts of sensation, perception, and observation, and psychologists and physiologists have investigated the mechanisms of perception. But while there has been steady progress in empirical discovery, there has not been parallel growth in conceptual clarity. Indeed physiological investigation has sometimes brought with it the temptation to conceptual confusion, which confusion has in its turn led to misinterpretation of the physiological findings.

To illustrate this we may briefly trace the history of the philosophy of sensation from its beginnings in the philosopher who was both the first systematic psychologist and the first systematic physiologist, namely Aristotle.

According to Aristotle sensation—sense-perception—is to be viewed as an interaction of the sensible object and the sensory capacity. When an animal hears a sound, sounding is the activity of the sounding object, hearing the activity of the animal's sense. And, according to Aristotle, these two activities are one and the same event: the sense and what is sensed are one in actuality.

Because of differences between Greek and English vocabulary, Aristotle's mysterious doctrine is easier to illustrate with an example such as taste. A piece of sugar, something which can be tasted, is a sensible object; my capacity for tasting is a sensitive potency; the operation of the sense of taste upon the sensible object is the same thing as the action of the sensible object upon my sense; that is to say, the sugar's tasting sweet to me is one and the same event as my tasting the sweetness of the sugar. The sugar is actually sweet, but until put into the mouth is only potentially tasting sweet. Medieval scholastics, codifying Aristotle, said that the sugar, outside the mouth, was sweet 'in first act' but not 'in second act'. It is the second actuality, sweetness in second act, which is at one and the same time the sugar's tasting sweet and the tasting of the sweetness of the sugar. (Something like black coffee, which can be made sweet if you put sugar into it, is not sweet either in first or second act, but only in potentiality.)

But it is not strictly correct, or strictly faithful to Aristotelian doctrine, to say, as I said above, that a piece of sugar is a sensible object, in the relevant sense. The presence or absence of sugar can of course be detected by the use of the senses; but the identification of the substance as *sugar* involves intellect as well as sense; and the real sensible object is the sweetness of the sugar, the sugar's sweet taste. It is this, and only this, of which it can plausibly be said that the actuality is identical with the taster's tasting. The actuality of *sugar*—that is to say the activities of which sugar, as such, is capable—clearly goes far beyond the activity of tasting sweet to a taster.

Indeed even among sensory qualities, such as colour, shape, and sweetness, it is important to make a distinction. We observed earlier that some qualities, such as sweetness and colour, can be detected only by a single sense, while others, such as shape and size, can be detected by more than one. It is only in the case of the qualities which are peculiar to individual senses that the Aristotelian theorem is plausible.

We can understand that the sweetness of X just is the ability of X to taste sweet. The quality is, of course, related to various chemical properties and constituents of X; but that relation, unlike the relation to the activity of tasting sweet, is a contingent one. The chemical features are the vehicle of the ability in which the secondary quality consists.

Aristotle had another thesis, which is connected with the theorem that the activity of a sensible property is identical with the activity of a sense-faculty. This is the thesis that the senses are never mistaken about their proper objects. The claim sounds extravagant. Is there any way in which it can be made plausible?

In recent philosophy it has often been stated that there is one—rather unexciting—sense in which it is impossible for the senses to be mistaken. Verbs like 'see', 'hear', and 'detect' have a feature which is sometimes described by saying that they are 'achievement verbs'. Just as it is impossible to win a fight unsuccessfully, since to win just is to fight victoriously, so, we are told, it is impossible to see incorrectly or hear mistakenly.

If one claims to have seen an eclipse or heard an explosion, one has to withdraw the claim if one is later persuaded that no eclipse or explosion took place. One has to retreat to saying 'I thought I saw . . .' or 'I thought I heard . . .'. But this does not mean that the faculties of sight or hearing are somehow infallible. Looking and listening may indeed be unsuccessful or misleading; but looking and listening are the tasks which if successfully carried out are dignified with the achievement verbs of perception.

Whatever the merits of this thesis, it is not what is meant by the Aristotelian theory of the infallibility of the senses about their proper objects. The traditional impossibility of mistaken sense-perception was restricted to such sense-objects as sounds and colours; it did not extend to the natures of the events or objects which were the causes or bearers of the sounds or colours. However, the claim that 'see' and 'hear' are achievement verbs applies as much to seeing dolphins as to seeing colours, as much to hearing cuckoos as to hearing noises.

At the other extreme, one may interpret the infallibility of the senses as meaning simply that if when you use your eyes you avoid making rash statements about how things are, and confine yourself to making statements about how things look to you here and now, then you cannot go wrong. Nor will there be any conflict between successive deliverances of a single sense: there is no conflict between a thing's looking to me at 5.15 from the north-north-west black and looking to me at 5.20 from the south-south-east white. But this infallibillity is purchased at too high a price: it is tantamount to accepting that the senses do not give us information about the world, but only about private sense-impressions.

In fact, the senses do give us information about the world, but they are not at all infallible. The traditional doctrine of the infallibility of the senses seems to be a mistaken way of stating the fact that the senses do have a special authority about the nature of their proper objects.

The senses are not infallible: it is not the case that whatever appears to a particular sense within its own competence is true. Not all statements made about colour on the basis of using our eyes are true: what appears to be red may not be red. Statements such as 'That is red' made on the basis of visual experience are not incorrigible. What is special about such sense-judgements is that they can be corrected only by a further use of the same sense. If we are not sure whether a thing really is the colour it looks from here to me now, we check by having a better look, by looking more closely, or looking in a better light. Against the verdict of any particular look an appeal lies; but where what is in question is colour, the appeal can never go to a court higher than that of sight.

With qualities proper to other senses, sight does not have the final verdict. A thing may look heavy, but I may correct this impression, and abandon any claim that it is heavy, by feeling its weight with my hand. So too with sense-properties that are detectible by more than one sense. A mistaken visual impression that something is round may be corrected by feeling; and conversely a mistaken tactile impression that something is round may be corrected by having a good look at it. So with motion, speed, number, and other things that are 'common sensibles' in the antique term—that is to say, perceptible by many senses. But with the proper sensibles, or the secondary qualities, the senses, though corrigible, can be corrected only by themselves. They are the final judges of their proper sensible, though they have to get into the right condition and position to judge.

In a similar manner, the theorem that the activity of a sensible property is identical with the activity of a sense-faculty seems to be strictly true only of secondary qualities like taste and colour; it is only of these that we can say that their only actualization, the only exercise of their powers, is the actualization of sense-faculties. A primary quality like heaviness can be actualized not only by causing a feeling of heaviness in a lifter, but also in other ways such as by falling and exerting pressure on inanimate objects.

We cannot say that the size or shape of an object simply is its ability to look big or to look round, or to feel round. It is true that I can see the shape of an object, just as I can taste the sweetness of an object. It is true that an object's looking round to me is the same as my seeing the roundness of the object to the same extent that the object's tasting sweet to me is the same as my tasting the sweetness of the object. But roundness cannot be identified with the ability to look round as sweetness can be identified with the ability to taste sweet. Nor can vision be identified with the ability to see roundness and squareness, to the same extent as taste can be identified with the ability to taste sweet, sour, salty, and bitter.

In modern philosophy the distinction between primary and secondary qualities took on great importance. Descartes, followed by many others since, believed that secondary qualities were not really properties of bodies at all. Heat, colours, and tastes, according to him, were strictly speaking mental entities or ideas. It was a mistake, he maintained, to think that if a body is hot it has some property like my feeling of heat, or that in a green object there was the same greenness as in my sensation. What we call colour, odour, flavour, sound, heat, and cold in external objects was merely the power those objects have to set our nerves in motion. In this view he is followed at the present time by many scientific psychologists and physiologists who would on other points claim to be rejecting Cartesian dualism.

Descartes' arguments for this theory are inconclusive. One is that the secondary qualities are perceived only by a single sense. But why should that mean that they are not objective? It is true that sense-impressions of such properties will not be corrigible by the exercise of another sense; and if a property is to be objective, then it must be possible to correct reports of the occurrence of such properties. But sense-impressions of second-ary qualities can be corrected in two ways: by further operation of the same sense by the same percipient; and by the co-operation of other observers using the same sense-faculty. Reports that an object is red may be shown to be false either by a closer look at the object or by the testimony of other observers.

A more important and influential argument was the claim that only primary qualities need to be attributed to things in order to give an adequate physiological account of sensation; and as sensation provides the only ground for asserting the existence of secondary qualities there is, therefore, no reason to accept their objectivity. Descartes pointed out that a bang on the head may cause one to see stars, stopping up the ears causes murmuring, cutting with a knife may cause pain. In all these cases we have sensation produced by mere motion. In the nerves which lead from the organs to the brain, he claimed, we find nothing but motion. Hence, he concluded, the external realities we call colour, odour, flavour, and so on, are only the powers that objects have to set our nerves in motion.

On Descartes' view what sees is the soul, not the eye, and the immediate act of seeing is located in the brain; for what a man sees is determined ultimately by the condition of his brain at the moment of seeing. He offers to explain the matter with the aid of analogies. Motions in the brain can cause sensation, just as letters written with the few characters of the alphabet can convey to us information about the most diverse scenes and produce a rich variety of emotions. A blind man, feeling his way with a pair of sticks, may find out much about the shape and position of objects that we find out with our eyes.

According to the Aristotelian view which Descartes' view was intended to supersede, it was not the soul nor the eye that saw but the whole animal. Moreover, there was a likeness of the thing sensed in the sense: there was a likeness of colour in sight and of flavour in taste. Green objects were really green, and secondary qualities were genuine properties of things, not mere ideas in the mind.

What is at issue in the question 'Are secondary qualities in objects *like* sensations'? If the question asks what things really look like when nobody is looking at them, then it is an obviously absurd question. No one wants to defend the theory that things are actually tasting sweet when no one is tasting them or actually looking pink when no one is looking at them. Aristotelian philosophers did believe that sugar untasted was actually, and not merely potentially sweet. But being actually sweet simply is to be potentially tasting sweet. To be sweet, in this sense, is to have the power to taste sweet to a tasting animal.

Philosophers who argue that secondary qualities are merely subjective are usually misled by confusing the notions of subjectivity and relativity. Many properties of substances are relative while being wholly objective. It is an objective matter whether Churchill was taller than de Gaulle, and it is an objective matter whether hemlock is poisonous. But of course 'being taller than de Gaulle' is a relational predicate, not an absolute one; and 'poisonous' in this context means 'poisonous to human beings'. The properties corresponding to these predicates are relative, but they are objective.

Another argument for the subjectivity of secondary qualities is based on the premiss that they do not exist unperceived. This premiss is in fact false. What is true is that secondary qualities are powers which are not exercised save when the qualities are perceived. This is precisely what was meant by the Aristotelian thesis that the sense and what is sensed are a single actuality, that sense and sense-object differ in potentiality but not in actuality.

It is correct that the secondary qualities are relative, that they are anthropocentric—or rather zoocentric. That is, they are powers to affect human beings and other animals in certain ways. But nothing follows from this about their being merely subjective; it is wrong to say that they are nothing in the object. The relation of the sensibilia to the sense-faculty is like the relationship of a key to a lock. A key's ability to fit a particular lock is something which is relative, but which is as objective as any fact about the key's size or shape.

What, in the last analysis, is the difference between the Aristotelian view and Descartes' view that secondary qualities are 'powers that objects have'? For Descartes the power was the power to set our nerves in motion; for the Aristotelians it was the power to produce likenesses of themselves. But the 'likeness' between the quality and the sensation is simply this: that the same word 'sweet' is the appropriate description both of the quality and of the sensation; and this in turn is because of the theorem of the identity in act of sense and sensation—the sugar's tasting sweet to me is the same event as my tasting the sweetness of the sugar.

In this the scholastics were more correct than Descartes: the felt qualities *can* be predicated of the objects themselves—the felt qualities, but not of course the feelings. Seeing red is totally unlike being red; but there is no reason to expect it to be alike, any more than to expect eating a potato to resemble being a potato, or knowing how to play the piano to resemble being a piano.

Descartes' most serious reason for thinking that redness could not be in the object was that it could be produced in the mind by other causes and because even when it was apparently in the object it could fail to reach the mind owing to interference with the nervous system. As we mentioned earlier, he argued that motions in the brain can cause sensation, just as letters written with the few characters of the alphabet can convey to us information about the most diverse scenes and produce a rich variety of emotions.

Let us take seriously Descartes' own analogy of letters and correspondence. Let us treat the information that reaches us via the senses from the world without as if it were a set of messages delivered by a postal service. The fact that a letter purporting to be written from a battlefield may be forged, or that letters genuinely written from battlefields may be intercepted, in no way shows that no letters can ever come from battlefields. Still less does it show that no letters are ever *about* battlefields. But that is what would be the analogy of secondary qualities being mere 'ideas in the mind' corresponding to nothing similar in the world without.

The Aristotelians were also correct against Descartes on the fundamental point that what senses is not the organ or the soul, but the whole animal. To discover whether an unknown animal has vision or not we have to study the behaviour of his whole body to ascertain whether he can discriminate between colours or between light and darkness.

Once again, Descartes can be corrected by an appeal to one of his own metaphors. He frequently compares the human body to a clock, and draws the analogy between a human being making a sense error with a clock telling the wrong time. To tell the wrong time is something that only a whole clock can do. The cause of the error may be in a particular part of the clock—say the escapement—but it is not the escapement which tells the wrong time, only the clock of which the escapement mechanism is a part. Similarly, though a sense error may be due to an indisposition or interference in a particular part of the body, it is the whole animal that makes the mistake. It is not that the soul sees what is misleadingly presented to it by the malfunctioning body; it is rather that the whole animal fails to see what is presented to it, because of a disorder in a part of it.

Descartes' philosophical errors about the nature of sense-perception were influential partly because in his empirical work he made a significant contribution to the science of optics. It was he, for instance, who first described accurately the nature of retinal images. He took an ox's eye and cut a window in the back of it, replacing the cut tissue with paper; holding the eye to the light he could see an inverted image of his room. This discovery was both an important contribution to optics, and the incidental source of considerable subsequent philosophical confusion.

One of the most bizarre, as well as the most ubiquitous, misunderstandings of the nature of the mind is the picture of mind's relation to body as that between a little man or homunculus on the one hand and a tool or instrument on the other. We smile when medieval painters represent the death of the Virgin Mary by showing a small-scale model virgin emerging from her mouth: but basically the same idea can be found in the most unlikely places.

Descartes, when first he reported the occurrence of retinal images, warned us not to be misled by the resemblance between images and their objects into thinking that when we saw the object we had another pair of eyes, inside the brain, to see the images. But he himself believed that seeing was to be explained by saying that the soul encountered an image in the pineal gland. This was a particularly striking version of what has been nicknamed 'the homunculus fallacy': the attempt to explain human experience and behaviour by postulating a little man within an ordinary man.

We humans are always inclined to explain things we only imperfectly understand in terms of the most advanced technology of the age we live in. As time passes and technology progresses the tool or instrument which the manikin is fancied to control gets more and more sophisticated. Thus Plato thought that the soul in its relation to the body could be compared with a sailor in a boat or a charioteer holding the reins. Many centuries later Coleridge said that what poets meant by the soul was 'a being inhabiting our body and playing upon it, like a musician enclosed in an organ whose keys were placed inwards' (*Letters*, Oxford, 1956, i. 278). More recently, the mind has been compared to a signalman pulling the signals in his signal box, or the telephone operator dealing with the incoming and outgoing calls in the brain. Most recently the boat, the chariot, the railroad, and the telephone exchange have given way to the computer, so that the relation of the soul to the body is envisaged as that of the programmer who writes the software to the hardware which executes the program.

What is wrong with the homunculus fallacy? In itself there is nothing misguided in speaking of images in the brain, if one means patterns in the brain which can be mapped on to features of the sensory environment. There is nothing philosophically objectionable in the suggestion that these schematic images may be observable to the neurophysiologist investigating the brain. What is misleading is to say that these images are visible to the soul, and that seeing consists in the soul's perception of the images.

The misleading aspect is that such an account pretends to explain seeing, but the explanation reproduces exactly the puzzling features which it was supposed to explain. For it is only if we think of the relation between a soul and an image in the pineal gland as being just like the relation between a human being and pictures seen in the environment that we will think that talk of an encounter between the soul and the image has any illuminating power at all. As a metaphor, manikin talk may be no more than a harmless necessary fancy; but as an element in a theory a manikin bedevils understanding. For whatever needs explaining in the behaviour of the man turns up, grinning and unexplained, in the shape of the manikin.

Contemporary psychologists know very much more than

Descartes did about the way in which information reaching the eyes is transmitted in coded form to the visual cortex. But they are still inclined to explain seeing by a version of the homunculus fallacy, saying that seeing consists in the brain's reading or decoding this information. Here, the little man looking at a picture has been replaced by the little man reading a book. Scientifically much has been learned; but philosophically there has been little advance. And the philosophical *naïveté* conceals the fact that what has been explained scientifically is not what seeing really consists in.

To see this, we must emphasize the difference between the containing of information (in the sense of communication theory) and the possession of knowledge. It is possible for a structure to contain information about a particular topic without having any knowledge about that topic. The train schedule contains the information about train departures; but it does not *know* what times the trains leave. The telephone cable contains the information which enables my wife in Oxford to hear and understand what I am saying in New York; but the telephone cable does not *know* even the sound, much less the content, of what I have to say to her.

A category difference is involved here. To contain information is to be in a certain state, while to know something is to possess a certain ability. A state (such as being a certain shape or size, or having a certain multiplicity or mathematical structure) is something describable by its internal, current, properties. An ability (such as the ability to swim across the English Channel or to produce a rabbit out of a top hat) is describable only by specification of what would count as the exercise of the capacity.

Knowledge is not a state but an ability and an ability of a unique kind. Knowledge no doubt has as its vehicle the containment of certain information; but it is not at all the same as the containment of the information. What extra is involved in knowing that *p*, over and above containing the information that *p*? If knowing that *p* is an ability, what is the exercise of that ability?

There is no simple answer. One cannot specify behaviour typical of knowing as one can specify behaviour typical of fear or anger. One cannot even specify behaviour typical of the possession of a particular piece of knowledge. Knowledge that Jones is approaching on the opposite side of the street will lead to different behaviour in the case of someone who finds Jones very good company and someone who regards him as a bore to be avoided at all costs. Knowledge that the dollar is overvalued with respect to the pound will be exercised in different behaviour on my part depending on whether I have dollars to sell or pounds to sell.

It is, of course, true that the verbal utterance of a sentence in a language is an activity which is uniquely expressive of the knowledge or belief articulated in that sentence. But there are many different languages in which the same belief can be articulated, and there is no guarantee that anyone who knows a particular item of information will ever utter it in any language at all.

Accordingly, there is no simple way of specifying how knowledge gets expressed in behaviour, and indeed some pieces of knowledge may never affect behaviour at all. The most that we can say is that to know is to have the ability to modify one's behaviour in indefinite ways relevant to the pursuit of one's goals. That may seem almost empty: but it is already enough to explain why the mere possession of information does not constitute knowledge. It is because the train schedule does not have any behaviour to be modified by what is written on it that it does not know what the train departure times are.

We introduced the consideration of knowledge in order to clarify the concept of seeing. Seeing—real seeing, as opposed to visual illusion—involves knowing. Indeed vision might be defined as the acquisition of knowledge in the visual mode. This definition is crude and also circular, since it leaves to be explained what is meant by 'the visual mode'. But for the moment we may ignore this, since it is the relation between seeing and knowledge which is our immediate concern.

In the Aristotelian tradition, prior to Descartes, it was insisted that it was not the eye that saw, nor the soul, but the whole animal organism. This was because the normal way to discover whether an animal sees is not just to study its eyes, but to investigate whether its behaviour is affected by changes of light and colour etc. Consequently, an explanation of seeing must be an explanation not only of the acquisition and storage of information, but also of what makes the containing of this information into knowledge—i.e. its relation to behaviour.

The study of vision in human beings must interconnect with

the study of language, since an important part of the behaviour which expresses visually acquired knowledge is linguistic behaviour. Normally, in an adult human being, the ability to see carries with it the ability to say what is seen, though of course not everything which is actually seen is talked about. The use of language to report what is seen, like any use of language, is remarkably free from stimulus control. No account of human perception can approach adequacy unless it includes an explanation of this fact.

Consequently, even if we knew every detail of the physiological processes by which visual information reaches the brain, and every detail of the physiological processes by which the linguistic utterance of visual reports is produced, the problem of the relationship between the input and the output would be completely untouched. But this problem is a major part of the problem which any physiological explanation of perception must solve.

The senses are discriminatory powers, powers for making distinctions and acquiring knowledge. This is the most important feature about sense-perception, the one which we must never forget. But the way in which I have been analysing the concept of sense-perception will have provoked in many readers a growing feeling of impatience, which must at long last be addressed.

When one defines vision as a power of visual discrimination, the philosopher in us rebels. Surely vision is the power to have *this* kind of experience, one thinks, and gestures towards whatever is currently in one's visual field. This may lead to a feeling of visual experiences as being a kind of film between us and the external objects which we see.

We have a strong inclination to feel that there is some irreducible element of knowledge in experience which cannot be known in any other way than by sensation. A blind man, we feel, cannot really understand what is meant by colour words. Of course, we make reports about our sensations, but we are inclined to think that no report of a sensation can ever be a full report, and that there must always be something that is unreportable. This feeling finds expression in reflections such as 'For all we know, what I call red is what you call green, and vice versa'. When I have a pain I may think that only I can really know how intense my pain is, or even that I am in pain at all.

This feeling we have of the incommunicability of sensation is an illusion. Whatever we know about our own sensations we can tell other people; what cannot be shared with others is not a piece of knowledge. 'Only I can know my sensation' means either that others cannot *know* that I am in pain; or that others cannot *feel* my pain. If it means the former then it is obviously false; someone who sees me falling into flames and screaming as my body burns knows perfectly well that I am in pain. If it means the latter then it is true but trivial, and there is no question of knowledge here. If 'Only I can feel my pain' is meant as a logical truth, it reveals the connection between *I* and *my*: *my* pain is precisely the pain that *I* feel. Equally, only I can sneeze my sneezes; my sneezes are the ones which I sneeze; but there is no temptation to think that there is something incommunicable about a sneeze.

Philosophical reflection may enable us to drive out pseudo-philosophical imaginings, such as the thought that what appears red to me may appear green to you and vice versa. But there remains a truth in the idea that vision is not just discrimination, not just the acquisition of information. We said earlier that it was the acquisition of information 'in the visual mode'. Can we put any flesh on that skeleton?

To have a sensation is not the same thing as to be in possession of a piece of knowledge. We do, of course, acquire information by the senses, but whatever information we acquire by the senses can be reported to others provided that they possess the appropriate language; and whatever can be reported to others can be discovered by others without the use of the sense in question, and without having the sensation. A blind man cannot see things, but he can learn all the things which others can learn by seeing, if only by asking others.

But sensation is not the same thing as the acquisition of information about sensible objects. The blind man can acquire the information, but he lacks the sense of sight. What is the distinction between the two? What is it to acquire the information not by testimony but through the visual mode? I know of no better way of making the distinction between sense-perception and information-gathering than the one Aristotle used long ago in the *De Anima*, where he says that 'where there is sense-perception there is also both pain and pleasure'.

The information acquired through the senses, and the

discriminations performed with their aid, may be acquired and performed by means other than the senses and indeed by agents other than human beings. A scanner might discover, and a computer tabulate, visual information about various human beings in order to sort them into categories according to their appearance. The visual features of landscapes can be catalogued by the kinds of apparatus used in lunar exploration. Such operations are not sense-perception because they occur without pleasure or pain: the human beings inventoried with all their statistics are not perceived as either beautiful or ugly, the landscapes strike neither terror nor awe.

Of course, not every sense-experience is either pleasant or painful; but a sense is essentially a modality for acquiring information in a modality which admits of pleasure and pain. The distinction between the intellectual knowledge that p and the sensation that p is to be sought, as Aristotle said, in the different relationship of each mode of cognition to pain and pleasure understood in the widest sense.

8

Imagination

By 'imagination' there are many things which we can mean. Let us begin by considering the imagination in the sense simply of the ability to call up mental images; an ability which you can exercise now simply by shutting your eyes and imagining what the White House looks like, or by sitting in silence and reciting the Lord's Prayer or a nursery rhyme to yourself.

Empiricist philosophers placed great importance on this ability, and regarded it as the essential element of human psychology; they thought that the scientific study of mental imagery by introspection would yield the key to the understanding of the mind. Behaviourist philosophers and psychologists in the present century have denied that introspection is a valid scientific method, and have devoted energy to showing that the phenomena of mental imagery are inadequate to perform the explanatory tasks which the empiricists assigned them.

I believe that the behaviourists are correct against the empiricists in both these contentions. However, it would be foolish to be led on—as some people have been—to deny the very existence of the imagination in the sense of the power to call up images. Here again, philosophical zeal to root out an error can lead to the denial of things which each of us knows very well to be true.

The imagination, in this sense, is a power that is generally shared by members of the human race. There is another sense of the word in which imagination is a much less evenly distributed faculty. The ability to imagine the world different in significant ways; the ability to conjecture, hypothesize, invent—this is a different form of imagination, creative imagination, possessed *par excellence* by persons such as poets, story-tellers, and scientists of genius.

I will call the imagination in the first sense the *fancy*, while reserving the word 'imagination' for the creative imagination.

Neither of these two kinds of imagination can be identified simply with the human intellect in the sense of the ability to master language.

The fancy confers on us the ability to talk to oneself; but this is a gift which is minor in comparison with the ability to talk at all. There could be a race just as intelligent as us which could think only aloud, and not in privacy; their lives would be both more honest and more noisy than ours, but there would be nothing in the world which would be beyond their ken without being also beyond ours.

But if the fancy is something inferior to the intellect, the imagination, in the second sense, is something superior to the intellect: it is the ability not just to understand language, but to use language creatively, to form new thoughts and discover new truths and build new worlds.

When we call up images in our fancy, they are very often images of things which we have seen and heard in the past. Events which have made a deep impression on us may have left behind vivid mental images; sometimes we recall these images and live once again through the stirring experiences we have had. Clearly, there is a close link between the fancy and the memory. Indeed, David Hume thought that both imagination and memory consisted simply in the reappearance of sense-impressions—a reappearance which took a more vivid form in the case of memory than in the case of imagination.

Hume's theory of memory is seriously deficient; but it is important to present a clear alternative account of the relationship between the memory, the intellect, and the two kinds of imagination which we have distinguished. To illustrate this distinction we can make use of a remarkable episode recorded in the life of Lord Macaulay. To while away a crossing of the Irish Sea, Macaulay repeated to himself the first five books of *Paradise Lost*. This feat was an exercise of memory, of intellect, and of fancy; but it was not an exercise of imagination.

Clearly, Macaulay performed a fantastic feat of memory; but had he found his way through a particularly complex maze after a single trial—as no doubt he would—this would have been equally a feat of memory without necessarily involving either intellect or fancy or creative imagination.

In so far as Macaulay understood and appreciated what he was reciting, he was exercising his intellect, in a way in which he would not have been had he merely been finding his way through a maze. For the understanding of *Paradise Lost* requires the use of one's knowledge of language with all its symbolic features.

Because Macaulay's whole performance went on under his breath, out of consideration for his fellow passengers on the steam packet, it was an exercise of the fancy—of the imagination in the more lowly sense of the word. Had he recited it aloud, it would have involved his intellect and memory without necessarily involving the fancy at all.

Finally, because *Paradise Lost*, unlike the *Lays of Ancient Rome*, was not Macaulay's own composition, what he did was not an exercise of the imagination in the grander sense in which that includes the faculty for artistic creation. While writing the *Lays* Macaulay was exercising his intellect and his creative imagination; but he was not exercising his memory. If he tried out various lines in his head, before writing them down, then he would have exercised his fancy. But, knowing what we do about Macaulay, we would not find it too surprising to learn that he wrote the poems verse after verse at high speed without any pause at all for meditation or reflection.

We will return later to consideration of the creative imagination. For the present I wish to dwell a little longer on the more humble faculty of the fancy. Philosophers of various schools have thought that the way to understand the nature of the fancy was to regard it as a special kind of sense: an inward or interior sense, unlike the five senses which faced outward. The theory of inner sense has been held by philosophers in many different traditions. It took, however, different forms within the different traditions. In one version of the Aristotelian tradition the inner sense of imagination was seen as active not only in the absence of external stimuli, but also whenever the outer senses themselves were active: the operation of the senses, on this interpretation, consisted in triggering off the imagination to produce the appropriate inner image. In the empiricist psychology of Hume, the deliverances of the outer senses are impressions, the deliverances of the inner senses are ideas; the whole content of our minds, the phenomenal base from which the whole of the world is to be constructed, consists of nothing but impressions and ideas.

Some philosophers have thought that the fancy was quite

literally a sense-faculty: it differed from outer senses like sight in having an organ and an object inside the body (in the brain) rather than an organ at the edge of the body (like an eye) and an object outside the body (like the trees I see). They have thought that when I conjure up a mental image, my relation to the image in my mind is similar to my relation to a picture I look at in an art gallery, except that in the one case I am looking at an inner image, and in the other case I am looking at an outer picture. Similarly, when I talk to myself *sotto voce* I hear with my inner ear words which I produce with my private voice, just as when I hold a conversation with you I hear with my outer ear words which you produce with your public voice.

One reason for viewing the imagination as an inner sense is this. Leaving aside the use of the word 'imagination' in which it means the creative faculty, there are many other uses of the word 'imagine' in English. Among the things which human beings do are (*a*) think of sensibilia in their absence, (*b*) make mental or verbal pictures of sensibilia, (*c*) acquire by the use of the senses misleading impressions and false beliefs about sensibilia, (*d*) wrongfully believe that they are using the senses about sensibilia.

All of these are sometimes described by the use of the verb 'imagine'. ('I often imagine you sitting at your desk', 'imagine the heavenly Jerusalem', 'It makes you imagine there is a colonnade there, but it is merely a skilful piece of *trompe-l'œil*', 'I thought I heard a knock at the door, but when I got there it turned out that I had just imagined it'.) There is a clear difference between the uses (*a*) and (*b*) on the one hand and the uses (*c*) and (*d*) on the other. The ability to think of sensibilia in their absence and to form images is very naturally called a faculty, and this is the faculty we have called the fancy. But it remains to be seen whether this faculty can be appropriately regarded as a sense.

When we use 'imagine' in uses (*c*) and (*d*), on the other hand, we seem to be talking of exercises of the ordinary exterior senses—unfortunate and infelicitous exercises; we are using the verb 'imagine' to report mistakes in perception, as in 'There isn't really a draught at all, it is just your imagination'. In these cases, of course, imagination is very like the operation of the senses. In fact it *is* the operation of the senses—the wrongful operation of the senses. But there is no 'faculty' of imagination here. The faculty that is being used—misused—is the sense-faculty in question. We have heard something quite different from the voluntary play of images in the head, which is the characteristic exercise of the fancy.

It would be absurd to say that the ability to do (c) and (d)—i.e. to make particular kinds of mistakes in and about the exercise of our sense-organs—is also a faculty. Surely there cannot be a faculty which consists in the fallibility of another faculty. This is brought out by the tale told of a philosopher—told in fact about more than one philosopher—who said that though his memory was beginning to fail him, his forgettery was in perfect working order.

However, the fact that the word 'imagine' in these uses is used to refer to genuine, if erroneous, operations of the senses is one of the reasons which have led philosophers to regard the imagination as an inner sense.

But if we reflect on the nature of the fancy, in connection with the employment of 'imagine' in the first two uses, we find that it is a faculty quite different from senses such as sight or smell or touch. The notion of an inner sense is a misleading one, in any of its historic versions. It exaggerates the superficial similarities between sensation and imagination, and conceals the profound conceptual differences between the two.

Sense-faculties—such as the senses of sight, hearing, taste, smell, and touch—are faculties for discriminating between public data which different subjects, depending on their circumstances, may be in better or worse positions to observe. The objects of imagination are created, not discovered; there is no such thing as gradual approximation to the optimal discernment of them. There can be no such thing as control by one observer on the acuteness of another's discrimination between phantasms. Imagination is not a peculiar kind of sensation; it is ordinary sensation phantasized. Imagination is phantasized sensation, and sensation is essentially discrimination; to imagine, therefore, is not to discriminate but to phantasize discrimination.

Sense-faculties characteristically operate by means of organs, that is, parts of the body which can be voluntarily controlled in ways which affect the efficiency of the discrimination. But the objects of the fancy are not perceived by organs. There is no organ which can be deployed to capture an image more vividly, as the eye may be screwed up to see more clearly, or the ear cocked to hear more sharply. Using one's fancy is not discriminating between images: it is phantasizing discrimination between objects.

There are other differences between the objects of sense and the objects of imagination. Mental images are not particular in the way in which sense-impressions are. I cannot see a tree which is no particular size but I may have a mental image of a tree without having a mental image of a tree of a particular size. I may imagine a woman without being able to answer such questions as whether the woman I am imagining is dark or fair. Any building must have a particular number of windows, even if the number is zero. But I may have an image of a building which has windows but no particular number of windows. I cannot find out how many windows my image of the Houses of Parliament has by counting them, as I can find out how many windows the Houses of Parliament have by counting them as I look at them.

There are various ways of being mistaken about what one is seeing in which one cannot be mistaken about what one is imagining: one cannot mistake an image of a bush for an image of a man as one can in suitable circumstances mistake a bush for a man. This is not meant to deny that people may say muddled or apparently inconsistent things about their mental images. In one breath a man may say that he has a picture of a page of poetry in his mind's eye, and in the next he may admit that he cannot read the page backwards. But this should not be interpreted as showing that he had misreported what was going on in his mind, but rather as throwing light on the difference between a mental image of a page of poetry, and a real page of poetry, or even for that matter a real picture of a page of poetry.

The fact is that a person's description of what he imagines enjoys a privileged status which is not shared by his description of what he sees. What makes my mental image of Napoleon an image of Napoleon is not that it looks like Napoleon, but that I say it is an image of Napoleon. Maybe, if I try to draw my image, it looks nothing like Napoleon. I have an image of Abraham, too, but neither I nor anyone else knows what Abraham looked like. None the less, when we are talking about my mental images, what I say goes.

It is, in fact, for this reason that there is a kind of justification for calling the fancy a sense. The power to have visual imagery depends on the ability to see. This is not a causal thesis: it does not mean that visual images can arrive in the mind, as a matter of contingent fact, only through a visual channel. Rather, the statement draws attention to the fact that the criterion for the occurrence of visual imagery is the report of the imaginer. Only someone who has mastered the use of language to describe visual appearances in the outside world can meaningfully use it in the description of his own fancy. So too with the other senses. This is the residue of truth in the theory that the fancy is an inner sense. But it also shows that it is truer to say that the imagination is part of the mind than to say that it is a sense.

Though the theory of the inner sense can be found both in Aristotelian and in empiricist psychology, there is a big difference between the way in which the relation between imagery and language was conceived by the two traditions. The empiricists believed that wherever there was thought there must be a flow of imagery. Aquinas, in the Aristotelian tradition, would not have disagreed: but for him it was not the images which gave content to the thought, but the thinking activity of the intellect which gave meaning to the images in the imagination.

Aquinas was correct, against the empiricists, in maintaining that when we think in images it is thought that confers meaning on the images, and not vice versa. We do much of our thinking by talking silently to ourselves; but the procession of imaged words through our imagination would not constitute a thought, would not have the meaning it does, were it not for our mastery of the language to which the words belong, a mastery which is an achievement of our intellectual power, not our image-making faculty.

If I call to mind the image of an advertisement in an unknown tongue, seen on a hoarding in a foreign city, the presence of that image in my mind does not mean that I have in my mind the thought the imagined words express. When our private thoughts are embodied not in imagined words, but in other visual or aural images, here too, as reflection will show, the image carries no unambiguous meaning on its face; to have meaning it must be employed in a particular way by the intellect. In the book of our thoughts, one might say, it is the intellect that is the author who provides the text; the imaging faculty is no more than typesetter and illustrator.

I made a distinction between the fancy and the imagination. I want to make a further subdivision within the realm of the creative imagination. Such imagination, I have maintained, is exhibited most conspicuously by geniuses both in science and in poetry. Both scientific and poetic imagination involves the use of language, in the framing of hypotheses or the construction of calculi no less than in the writing of verse or drama.

However, when Darwin framed the hypothesis of evolution by natural selection, or when Cantor invented transfinite arithmetic, they did not need to use language in any non-literal manner. But it is one of the characteristics of the literary imagination that it is intimately linked with the ability to use language figuratively, in symbolic images. So that the literary imagination is called 'imagination' by a double title.

Linguistic imagination is exercised, of course, not only by advanced practitioners of science and literature. Everyone who uses language to make a supposition or frame a conjecture is using imagination. So too is a parent inventing a bedtime story or a child playing consequences at a birthday party. The role playing of children typically involves both linguistic and non-linguistic elements, whether they are pretending to be jousting knights or doctors treating patients. The exercise of this kind of imagination does not even look as if it were the operation of an inner sense; but its links with the more sophisticated craft of the dramatic poet are obvious.

Not only poets, but prophets and divines have claimed that there is a special link between their calling or craft and its expression in imagery. Sometimes the claim takes the following form. Language in its literal sense is adapted to cope with material objects, with bodily entities. But the poet, the prophet, the divine, are concerned with matters spiritual, not bodily. Therefore they can use language only figuratively. An argument of this form sometimes seems to underpin the statements of theologians who tell us that religious discourse is of its nature analogical. This theory sometimes takes the form of presenting analogy as being a form of acquiring knowledge about God: thus the linguistic imagination gets presented as a cognitive faculty.

The imagination is clearly not a means of acquiring information about the world outside us in the way that the senses are. One cannot discover the way the world is simply by imagining. None the less there is a sense in which we can increase our knowledge of things by using our imagination. It is similar to the way in which we can learn to see things better by drawing them or modelling them. Using our imagination can increase our sensitivity to other people and thus our ability to inform ourselves about what they feel and are likely to do. Works of the imagination may teach us things about human beings; great works of fiction are means by which the human race extends its self-awareness. Could we say that knowledge of God could be acquired by the use of the imagination, in the way our knowledge of ourselves and of our peers grows through story-telling and poetry?

For imagination to be a genuine source of knowledge there has to be some way of distinguishing what is discovered by the imagination from what is created by the imagination. How can we settle whether God is discovered by the imagination or created by it? After all, if there is no God, then God is incalculably the greatest single creation of the human imagination. No other creation of the imagination has been so fertile of ideas, so great an inspiration to philosophy, to literature, to painting, sculpture, architecture, and drama; no other creation of the imagination has done so much to stir human beings to deeds of horror and nobility, or set them to lives of austerity or endeavour. But the very fact that an atheist can salute the idea of God as a magnificent work of the human imagination shows that whether God exists is something which the imagination itself cannot settle.

The creative imagination, I said earlier, is not something which can be contrasted with the intellect in the way in which the fancy can: it is one aspect of the intellectual faculty. In the case of any substantial intellectual structure, the question whether it is to be attributed to imagination or to insight, whether it is to be saluted as a creation or discovery, is a question which cannot be settled by looking within the mind or examining the expression in language of the intellectual structure. It depends on whether the structure can be regarded as a true account of the world.

Thus, the apparatus of the human mind described by Freud is something whose description does credit to Freud's imaginative genius; but whether it really describes the human mind in a scientific way, or is a newly created mythology, is something which has to be settled outside the realm of the imagination. Darwin and Freud clearly shared a variety of imaginative gifts: the ability to conceive novel principles of explanation, the skill to embody these principles in lucid and lively prose, the courage to challenge fashions of scientific orthodoxy. But it is possible to agree that the two possessed extraordinary imagination, and yet to believe that one but not the other possessed genuine scientific insight.

This double aspect of the intellectual imagination can be observed not only in regard to theology and to science, but within the realm of philosophy itself. The value which one places on the intellectual gifts of Descartes, for instance, depends on whether one accepts or rejects Cartesianism. Paradoxically, his genius appears greater to those who regard his doctrines as totally erroneous. Those who accept a Cartesian view of the mind can, of course, admire Descartes for being the first person to state certain elemental truths with cogency and elegance and concision. But only one who is cured of Cartesianism can fully be awed by the breathtaking power of an intellect which could propagate, almost unaided, a myth which to this day has such a comprehensive grasp on the imagination of a large part of the human race.

9

The Intellect

In Chapter 2 we said that in its primary sense the mind is the capacity to acquire intellectual abilities. It is a capacity, not an activity: babies have minds even though they do not yet exhibit intellectual activities. It is a second-order capacity: an ability to acquire or possess abilities. To know a language is to have an ability: the ability to speak, understand, and perhaps read the language. To have a mind is to have a capacity one stage further back: the ability to acquire abilities such as the knowledge of a language.

The mind, I said, is the capacity to acquire intellectual abilities, that is to say, abilities for intellectual activities. Intellectual activities are ones which involve the creation and utilization of symbols. Mathematics, philosophy, portrait painting, and poetry are clearly intellectual activities by this definition. The definition, you will have observed, has an indistinct borderline; this is a merit of the definition, since the concept it is aimed to capture is a fuzzy concept.

The intellect is often defined as the capacity for thought. This definition is, in essentials, correct, but if it is not misleading it needs investigation and qualification. What are the essential features of thought? Suppose that I think of a dragon. There seem to be two things which make this thought the thought it is: first, that it is a thought of a dragon and not of a horse or an eagle; secondly, that it is my thought and not your thought or Queen Elizabeth's thought. These seem to be the two essential properties of any thought: to have a content and to have a possessor. Of course, thoughts may have other properties too— e.g. they may be profound or childish, exciting or depressing, and so on—but the two things essential to any thoughts seem to be that they should be somebody's thoughts and that they should be thoughts of something.

We employ the word 'think' in two quite different ways: we

talk of thinking *about* something, and we talk of thinking *that* something. Thus, in the first way we may say that someone abroad thought of home, or thought of his family; in the second way we may say that someone thought that there was a prowler downstairs, or that there was likely to be an increase in the rate of inflation. In one usage, but not in the other, the verb introduces an indirect speech construction. We might, if we wished, call thoughts reported in these two different ways different kinds of thought: thinking *of* and thinking *that*. This would be a little misleading, because thinking *that* involves thinking *of* (you cannot think that inflation will increase without thinking of inflation) and because thinking of X is usually thinking *that* X something-or-other (as thinking of the family may take the form of thinking that the family will just now be sitting down to breakfast). So it is probably preferable to make this distinction as a linguistic one between two uses of 'think' rather than between two types of thought.

Thought has a property which philosophers have called 'intentionality'. Intentionality is the relationship which thought has to that which the thought is about. Philosophers have tried to bring out the special nature of this relationship in several ways, by considering the semantic properties of verbs and constructions used to report thoughts.

First, they have made a contrast between intentional and non-intentional verbs. Suppose we compare the verb 'think of' with the verb 'burn'. If I want to discover whether you have burnt the toast, I need to look at the toast. If I want to discover whether you are thinking of the toast, it is no use to investigate the toast; I need to find out from you. A non-intentional verb like 'burn' reports a change in the object of the action it reports; an intentional verb like 'think of' reports a change in the subject. Intentional actions are actions which do not bring about any change in their objects.

Secondly, it has been pointed out that the objects of intentional actions and states need not exist at all. 'Jesus will come again' can only be true if there is such a person as Jesus; not so 'Paul believes that Jesus will come again'. This is a particular instance of a more general feature: referring expressions which occur inside the contexts which are created by intentional verbs do not refer to objects in the world in the way in which referring expressions do outside such contexts. The contexts created by intentional verbs are, in the philosophers' jargon, 'referentially opaque'.

What this means can be illustrated by an example. Suppose that two expressions both refer to the same individual, as 'Cicero' and 'Tully' do. Then, in general, if you take a sentence containing one expression and replace the expression with the other expression, the sentence will retain its truth-value. 'Tully wrote many speeches' is true just as 'Cicero wrote many speeches' is true; 'Tully died in his bed' is false just as 'Cicero died in his bed' is false. But this general rule will no longer hold if the sentence in question contains an intentional verb in a crucial position. Take the sentence 'Caiaphas believed that Messiah had not yet come'. This true sentence becomes false if we substitute 'Jesus' for 'Messiah', even if Jesus is indeed Messiah.

Philosophers have attempted to use these, and other semantic features of psychological verbs such as 'think', 'believe', in order to give a formal definition of intentionality, and thus display unambiguously a logical structure which distinguishes the mental from the physical. The task is a difficult one, and may indeed prove impossible. This is not because there are no differences of logical importance between sentences reporting physical events and those reporting mental events and states. It is rather that there is such a variety of verbs, expressions, and constructions which are used in reporting our mental life that it is rash to hope that one or two generalizations will suffice to characterize logical features which are common to all of them and which yet distinguish them from all others.

In this chapter, instead of seeking a formal definition of intentionality, I will try to illustrate the feature in connection with different mental states and activities. We may begin by returning to the consideration of thought and thinking. I said a little while ago that one cannot think that X will do such and such without thinking of X. This statement perhaps involves a slight tightening up of ordinary usage. For sometimes we use 'A thinks that *p*' as a synonym for 'A believes that *p*'; and of course one can have a belief without that belief's occupying one's thought, and without thinking of the content of the belief at a particular moment. The sense of 'think' of which my remark is

true is that in which 'think' is related to 'believe' as episode to
disposition. In this sense 'think' has a continuous tense: 'A is
thinking that p'. In this respect 'think' differs from 'believe'
because one cannot say 'A is believing that p'. Though ordinary
usage does not mark the distinction sharply, for philosophical
purposes it is convenient to reserve the word 'think' for the
episode, and use 'belief' for the disposition. Thinking out a
problem, and thinking of something, are both clearly episodic,
and therefore match with the episodic sense of 'thinking that'.

So much, initially, for the relation between thinking and
believing. What of the relation between thinking and saying?
Crudely, one could say that thinking is an abstraction from
saying, and believing is an abstraction from thinking. But if this
crude summary is not to be misleading, the relationships must
be examined more closely.

Not all thoughts are given public expression in words. I may
say to myself, behind clenched teeth, 'What a frightful bore this
man is!' while being deterred by politeness from letting such a
thought show. Partly for this reason, it is natural to regard
thinking that p as a kind of internal saying that p; and this, if
rightly understood, is correct. But thinking that p is not simply
saying 'p' to oneself in one's head.

Some thoughts are not put into words even in the privacy of
the imagination: the wanderer's thought of his family at
breakfast may be simply an image of them sitting in the kitchen,
not the internal enunciation of any proposition. On the other
hand, one can say 'p' to oneself quite insincerely—in one's head
but not in one's heart, to use the formula of Trollope quoted in
Chapter 2. We can say that thinking that p is tantamount to
saying in one's heart that p provided that we do not think that
saying in the heart must involve silent monologue or subvocal
mouthing.

When a person has the thought that p, the content of the
thought has the same complexity as the sentence which would
give it expression if he expressed the thought. This is not to be
regarded as a remarkable parallelism discoverable by armchair
psychology; it is simply that we have no criteria for the
simplicity or complexity of thoughts other than the criteria for
the simplicity or complexity of the words and sentences that
give them utterances. Whenever I think that something is the

case there is always a form of words that would express the content of my thought: that is guaranteed by the indirect speech construction, since the *that*-clause, suitably modified, will provide the necessary form of words. It is the relationship between thought and its expression which gives rise to the features which philosophers have attempted to use in order to define intentionality.

The special logical features of the description of mental states correspond to the special logical features which attach to the use of words to quote a statement made by someone else rather than to make a statement in one's own right. Thus, if I say 'The toast is burnt' I am making a statement about the toast; if I say 'You said "the toast is burnt" ' I am making a statement about you. In the statement 'Jesus will come again' the word 'Jesus' refers to Jesus; in the statement 'Paul said "Jesus will come again" ' the word 'Jesus' does not refer to Jesus; if it refers at all, it refers to a word uttered by Paul.

The thesis that the intellect is the capacity for thought is a true thesis if the word 'thought' is taken in the sense which we have illustrated. That is to say, the intellect is the capacity to have states of mind which display the complex intentionality which finds expression in articulate language.

If the intellect is the capacity for thought, how can it be said that the intellect is a capacity which is not shared by other animals? Surely a dog, when he sees his master take the lead off the hook on the door, thinks that he is going to be taken for a walk and expresses the thought in a very clear manner by leaping and bounding about and pawing at the door. No doubt there are certain thoughts—about history, poetry, or mathematics, for instance—which are beyond the capacity of dumb animals; but it surely cannot be claimed that the capacity for thought itself is peculiar to human beings.

It is indeed true that animals can have simple thoughts. The thoughts that we attribute to them are of course expressible in language—the indirect speech construction guarantees that. But for a thinker to have a thought it is not necessary that the thinker himself be able to express it in the language in which we would express it. But this shows how the original definition of the intellect as the capacity for thought needs to be modified. The intellect is the capacity for thinking those thoughts that only a language-user can think. And thoughts that only a language-user can think are thoughts for which no expression in non-linguistic behaviour can be conceived: e.g. the thought that truth is beauty, or that the stars are many light years away.

Earlier, I suggested that when we say that a dog wants his master to open the door for him, we are not attributing to the dog our human concepts of 'master' and 'door'; all we need mean is that in his repertoire of concepts there is one which picks out the object we pick out by 'master' and one which picks out the object we pick out by 'door'. When we attribute simple thoughts to animals we have an extreme case of the opacity which affects our use of language when we apply the indirect speech construction to other human beings.

Earlier we said that the essential features of thought were that they should have a possessor and a content. Problems arise both about the identification of the possessor of the thought and about the content of the thought.

What is the relation between a thought and its content? What makes a thought of X a thought of X? Does a thought become a thought of X by being like X? Or is there some other relationship? How can it be a relationship at all, since we can have thoughts of what does not exist, like my thought of a dragon, and there is nothing in such a case for my thought to be related to? Moreover, even if we could agree on the nature of the relationship—say resemblance—and concentrate on the cases where there are things to be related to—say horses—there is still the problem: what *has* the relationship? A statue of a horse is a piece of stone or bronze resembling, with greater or less success, a real horse; but in the mind there is nothing corresponding to the stone or the bronze to bear the resemblance.

If we turn from thoughts *of* to thoughts *that*, this problem seems compounded. No doubt the thought that the cat is on the mat may be said to resemble the cat's being on the mat in that it must have the same abstract structure, sharing the complexity of the state of affairs it represents. But even if we say that the elements of the thought must stand to each other in the same relationship as the elements of the state of affairs, the problems recur: what if there is no such state of affairs, and how is each element of the thought related to each element of reality?

So much, for the moment, for the problem of identifying the content of a thought. The second major problem concerns the identity of the possessor of the thought. If A thinks of a horse, what makes A's thought of a horse A's thought? There is nothing in the content of a thought which makes it one person's thought rather than another. (Even when Napoleon thought to himself 'I am Napoleon' there was nothing in the content of the thought to distinguish it from the thought 'I am Napoleon' in the mind of a deluded twentieth-century Irishman.) Innumerable people beside myself believe that two and two make four: when I believe this what makes the belief *my* belief?

The answer to these problems is in one way simple, in another impossibly complicated. Both the content and the possessor of a thought are given by the expression of a thought. The possessor of a thought is the person who expresses it; the content of a thought is what its possessor would intelligently and sincerely say if asked what she was thinking. This simple answer is correct: but immediately questions crowd in demanding further answers. What of thoughts that are not expressed? Can the notions of intelligence and sincerity here be spelt out without circularity? Surely speech is only intelligent if accompanied by thought, and the test of the sincerity of an utterance is that it should match the thought behind it.

Let us develop the first objection. Are there not unexpressed thoughts, the thoughts which pass through our mind in private, unvoiced, thinking? Indeed there are, and we may well ask: what makes these thoughts my thoughts? It may seem unhelpful, though it is true, to reply: they are thoughts which, if they were expressed, would be expressed by me. To make this answer seem less vacuous, and to convince ourselves that even in this case the criterion for the possessor is bodily, we should reflect on cases of alleged thought-reading or telepathy.

Suppose that at a thought-reading session, or seance, the thought-reader or medium says 'Someone in this room is thinking of Eustace'. Here, *ex hypothesi*, the occurrence of the thought has been ascertained through means other than normal bodily communication. Even here, the way we would seek to decide whether what the thought-reader said was *true* would involve appeal to bodily criteria. What settles the matter is whose hand goes up, whose voice confesses to the private thought. And *whose* the hand is, *whose* the voice is, is determined by looking to see which body is involved.

Let there be no misunderstanding here. I asked the question:

what makes my thoughts *my* thoughts; I gave the answer: my thoughts are the thoughts which are expressed by my body. In saying this I am not suggesting that it is by observing actual or conjecturing hypothetical movements of my own body that I decide which thoughts are my own thoughts. There is no decision here; I know without any intermediary what I am thinking. There is no conceivable state of mind during which I know that certain thoughts are present, and wonder whose thoughts they are, mine or someone else's. It is not by bodily criteria that I know which thoughts are mine, or know what it is that I am thinking, because it is not by any criteria at all that I know these matters. But what it is that I know, when I know that certain thoughts are mine, is the same thing as other people know; and what I know, and what they know, is something to which the bodily criteria are necessarily relevant.

Now let us turn to the second problem: what determines the content of our thoughts? Many of our thoughts are conducted in language, and all our thoughts are expressible in language. The question 'how do our thoughts have content?' is the same as the question 'how do our words have meaning?'

Indeed, the crucial role of the intellect is to convey meaning on the words we use; to provide the understanding of language which enables us to speak meaningfully. How does the intellect achieve this?

We are tempted, when first we begin philosophy, to think of meaning and understanding as processes which are simultaneous with, and accompany, the speaking, hearing, and writing of language. Unlike the written or spoken syllables, so we are tempted to think, the elements of these processes are invisible and inaudible; the processes are not material, but take place in the spiritual recesses of the mind.

Before seeking to answer the question whether meaning and understanding are mental processes, we should try to get clearer what we mean by 'mental process', and whether there are items which could be appropriately described by the expression. Pause a moment in reading, take your eyes from the paper, and recite the alphabet to yourself without moving your lips and without making any sound. This is something which could well be described as a mental process. It is mental in the sense that it is something 'done in your head'; it is not in any ordinary way perceptible to others, unlike reciting the alphabet aloud; it is only by asking you that someone who came into the room while you were engaged in it could find out what you were doing. It is a process in the sense that it takes time, a time which could be measured on a stop-watch; it has a beginning, a middle, and an end, and could be interrupted, for instance if the telephone rang before you had got past 'K'; it can be simultaneous with public processes: you might have a bet with yourself that you could get to the end of it before the match you are holding in your fingers burns out.

Understanding and meaning are not mental processes of this kind. The criteria by which we decide whether someone understood a sentence, and what he meant by it, are quite different from the criteria by which we discover what mental processes are going on while someone is talking or writing. Understanding a sentence is not a process that accompanies the sentence; when I am half-way through uttering a sentence, that does not mean that I am half-way through understanding it. We cannot say that understanding is a momentary event, either. When would the event of understanding occur? At the end of the sentence? Then did we utter the sentence before we understood what it meant? At the beginning of the sentence? Then do we always know when we start a sentence how we are going to end it? And if we do not does that mean that we do not understand what we are saying?

Of course there can be mental processes which accompany the utterance of a sentence. As I try to make my simple point clear to my colleagues on the committee, my tenth utterance of my proposition may be accompanied with mounting feelings of impatience and indignation. While I am typing a confidential letter of reference I may think to myself 'Damn! I forgot to get that new typewriter ribbon yesterday'. But there is no process of this kind, accompanying my production of a sentence, which can be regarded as my understanding of the sentence.

If meaning was a mental process accompanying the utterance of a sentence, it should be possible for the process of meaning to take place without the sentence being uttered at all. Can one, in fact, perform the act of meaning without uttering the sentence? If you try to do so, you are likely to find yourself reciting the sentence itself under your breath. But of course it would be absurd to suggest that simultaneously with every public utterance of a sentence there is a private one too: it would surely take great skill to ensure that the two processes were exactly synchronized with each other! And how terrible if the two came slightly out of synchrony, so that the meaning of one word got mistakenly attached to the next one!

Moreover, the question whether somebody understands a sentence, and whether she really means it, can be raised about sentences uttered in the privacy of the imagination no less than about sentences uttered before a public audience. Infuriated by a curmudgeonly relation, I may mutter to myself 'I wish he would drop dead!' Luckily, I don't really mean it. I hum in my mind a Russian folk-song, enchanted by the sound of the words. But I haven't the faintest idea what they mean. If understanding and meaning were processes, they would have to accompany private utterances as well as public utterances. So if the processes involved were some kind of inner utterance, we would be set off on an endless quest for the real understanding.

Some philosophers have thought that understanding was a mental process in rather a different sense. They have conceived the mind as a hypothetical mechanism postulated to explain the observable intelligent behaviour of human beings. If one conceives the mind in this way one thinks of a mental process, not as something comparable to reciting the ABC in one's head, but as a process occurring in this special mental machinery. The process on this view is a mental process because it takes place in a medium which is not physical; the machinery operates according to its own mysterious laws, within a structure which is not material but spiritual; it is not accessible to empirical investigation, and could not be discovered, say, by opening up the skull of a thinker.

Such processes need not, on this view, be accessible either to the inner eye of introspection: the mental mechanism may operate too swiftly for us to be able to follow all its movements, like the pistons of a railway engine or the blades of a lawn mower. But we may feel that if only we could sharpen our faculty for introspection, or somehow get the mental machinery to run in slow motion, we might be able actually to observe the processes of meaning and understanding.

Perhaps few people will admit to believing that the mind is a field of paramechanical causes when the hypothesis is candidly set out before them. At most they may claim, without great plausibility, that talk of mental mechanisms is intended merely as a temporary and abstract way of referring to the physiological mechanisms of the brain. But the two different senses of 'mental process' are often combined in a manner which generates further confusion.

For instance, a philosopher may postulate a mental event as part of a theory of human behaviour: he may, for instance, claim that a voluntary action is an action which is preceded by an act of willing. It soon becomes obvious that in the case of most of our voluntary actions we are not conscious of any preceding mental events which could be described as 'acts of willing'. The philosopher, unwilling to relinquish his theory, suggests that the event did occur—it was an item in the history of the mind— but it was too sudden, or too brief, to be properly observed by introspection. It may even be suggested that it was not ever presented to consciousness at all, but took place in the subconscious, this being thought of as being the underside, or backside, of the mental mechanism.

According to one version of the mental-mechanism doctrine, understanding the meaning of a word consists in calling up an appropriate image in connection with it. In general, of course, we have no such experience when we use a word and in the case of many words (such as 'the', 'if', 'impossible' 'million') it is difficult even to suggest what would count as an appropriate image. But let us waive these points, allow that perhaps we can have images in our mind without noticing that we do, and consider only the kind of word for which this account sounds most plausible, such as colour words. We may examine the suggestion that in order to understand the command 'Bring me a red flower' one must have a red image in mind, and that it is by comparison with this image that one ascertains which flower to bring. This cannot be right: otherwise how could one obey the order 'imagine a red patch'? Whatever problems there are about identifying the redness of the flower recur with identifying the redness of the patch.

It is of course true that when we talk, mental images often do pass through our minds. But it is not they which confer meanings on the words we use. It is rather the other way round: the images are like the pictures illustrating a text in the book. In general it is the text which tells us what the pictures are of, not the pictures which tell us what the words of the text mean.

In fact, understanding cannot be thought of as a process at all. Understanding is a kind of ability, and therefore is a state rather than a process. In so far as the exercise of understanding is an exercise of intelligence, we may call understanding a mental state. But it is important to guard against misunderstanding here. Understanding may be a mental state, but it is not a psychological state like pain or depression or excitement. Such states last over periods, and can be continuous or interrupted; but one cannot know uninterruptedly what a word means.

Understanding is not a process or event; but the acquisition and the exercise of understanding may be a process or an event. The function of the intellect is sometimes described as being able to acquire and exercise abstract ideas. What is an abstract idea? Well, it might be said, the abstract idea of *cat* is an idea of cat which does not involve the size or shape or colour of any particular cat. But what is the use of such an idea? Since there can be no actual cat without size or shape or colour, will not an intellect which operates by means of abstract ideas distort reality in the very process of grasping it? Surely a thought which thinks a thing otherwise than it is must be a false thought.

To evaluate the process of intellectual abstraction, one must disentangle the ambiguity of the last sentence of the previous paragraph. To think a thing *to be* otherwise than it is is certainly to think falsely. But if all that is meant by 'thinking a thing otherwise than it is' is that the way it is with our thinking is different from the way it is with the thing we are thinking about, in its own existence, then there need be no falsehood involved. To think that Henry VIII had no weight would be to think a false thought; but there is no falsehood involved in thinking of Henry VIII without thinking of his weight. Henry VIII could never exist without having some weight or other, but a thought of Henry VIII can certainly exist without any thought at all about his weight.

Abstraction, perhaps, is not as such peculiar to intellectual cognition. After all, Henry VIII's dog could smell Henry VIII without smelling his weight, even though he could not smell a king who had no weight. None the less, human beings have a special abstractive power which is not shared by animals. In order to possess the type of concepts which we human adults use to refer to and describe the objects of our experience it is not at all sufficient merely to have sensory experience. Children see, hear, and smell dogs before they acquire the concept *dog* and learn that the word 'dog' can be applied to labradors, poodles, and dachshunds but not to cats and sheep. Animals share with human beings the experience of pain, and human beings feel pain from birth, and perhaps before birth; but humans acquire the concept pain when they learn language. Children feel pricks and aches and cramps long before they learn to call them, but not tickles and itches, by the name 'pain'.

The family pets live in much the same sensory environment as the family baby: the baby, but not the pets, learns from what is to be seen and heard the mastery of symbols to describe and change that environment. Concept-formation cannot be regarded simply as a residue from sense-experience. A special ability unshared by animals is necessary if human beings are to acquire concepts from the experience which they share with animals.

Is the acquisition of concepts appropriately described by the word 'abstraction'? Is it true to say that concepts are abstracted from experience? Two separate doctrines may be expressed in these terms. The first is that concepts and experiences stand in a certain causal relation; the second is that they stand in a certain formal relation.

In the causal sense, to say that concepts are abstracted from experience is to say either that experience is a sufficient causal condition, or that it is a necessary causal condition for the acquisition of concepts. We have already argued against the contention that it is sufficient condition. How far it is a necessary condition seems to be partly an empirical matter and partly a philosophical question. It is an empirical matter, for instance, to discover how much a blind man might learn of a textbook on optics. It is a philosophical question how far mastery of such a textbook would count as possession of the concepts of colour without, for example, the ability to match colours against colour samples.

Concepts may be said to be abstract not in the causal sense that they are abstracted from experience but in the formal sense that they abstract from experience. That is to say, they are abstract in comparison with experiences. Sense-experience is always of a particular experience; intellectual conception, as such, is of the universal. This formal relationship is distinct from the causal relation; it would remain even if universal concepts were not acquired from experience. Even innate ideas would still be more abstract than representations of individuals, whether these were themselves acquired or innate.

For to have the concept of dog is not to be able to recognize or think of a particular dog with particular characteristics. It is *inter alia* to be able to recognize any dog no matter what its particular characteristics, to think about dogs without necessarily attributing particular characteristics to them, and to know general truths about dogs as such. And this is true no matter whether the concept of dog is inborn or acquired by experience.

In contemporary philosophical usage 'concept' has two contrasting uses. In the one sense, a concept is something subjective: to possess a concept is to have mastered a skill, for instance to have mastered the use of a word. It is in this sense that the word has been used in the discussion up to this point.

In another sense, concepts are something objective. Some philosophers have said that concepts are the reference of predicates. In the sentence 'Eclipse is a horse', for instance, just as the name 'Eclipse' stands for a horse, so the predicate '. . .is a horse' stands for a concept—and a concept is not something in anybody's mind, but something as objective as a mathematical function. If this is true, then the acquisition of a concept in the former sense consists in some kind of contact with, or grasp of, the concept in the objective sense: the universal *horse*, the property of *horsiness*, or the reference of the predicate '. . . is a horse'. This philosophical thesis is often given the name 'realism'.

It is an enormous task, which will not be undertaken here, to evaluate the claims of philosophical realism. I will merely mention, without defending, the account of the nature of concepts which I personally find most attractive: it is one which is a development of the treatment of intentionality by medieval philosophers.

According to this theory, a thought is an actualization of two different potentialities: it is the actualization of the mind's power to think, and of the thinkability of objects of thought. (This corresponds to the point made earlier that the two essential elements of a thought are that it has a possessor and a content.) The actuality of the object of thought is the same as the actuality of the power of thinking. This arcane doctrine had a very simple meaning. The intellect just is the capacity for intellectual thought (for doing such things as making universal judgements about horses). The object of intellectual thought, the universals such as *horsiness*, have no existence outside thought. They are just the capacity of non-universals to be brought within the scope of the intellect's generalizing ability.

Material objects in the world—real horses such as Eclipse—are of course not to be identified with universals. These are objects which are potentially thinkable; and their thinkability, their intelligibility, is their capacity to be brought under the universal concepts of the intellect's creation.

On this view, the two kinds of concepts are facets of the same reality. The horsiness of Eclipse (that is to say, Eclipse's life as a horse) has existence outside thought; it has its own history and causal interactions; but the universal *horse*, horsiness as such, has no existence outside thought. Horsiness indeed is not something I think *of* in the way that I think of Napoleon; it is something, rather, which I think when I think of horsiness without thinking of the horsiness of any particular object. The thinkability of the horsiness of Eclipse is its ability to be abstracted by the human abstractive power, the human ability to classify and describe by the predicates of human language. And the most significant characteristic of human language is precisely its universality. the ability which it confers for the recognition of laws which go beyond the present in space and time and even for the formulation of truths which claim necessary and timeless validity.

Plato and his followers have argued that if the mind can know the eternal and the changeless, then the mind must itself be in essence eternal and changeless. At the very least they claim, it must be an immortal entity that can survive the death of the body. To reach this conclusion Plato needs not only the premiss that the mind is the capacity to know the eternal, but also the premiss that like can only be known by like. Is there any truth in this archaic thesis? Well, if something is to be said to have knowledge of the multiplication table, it must be capable of an output isomorphic to the multiplication table. But the thesis that the knower must have the same properties as the known is plausible only of the formal or structural properties of the knowledge and its object. Knowledge that p is the case must resemble the state of affairs that p to this extent, that 'p' is both the appropriate description—indeed the identifying description—of the state of affairs and is the appropriate expression— indeed the identifying expression—of the item of knowledge. But this concerns the content of knowledge and not the mode of knowing; the matter to be represented and not the manner of representation. The Platonists have never provided any good reason for thinking that there cannot be fugitive acquaintance with unchanging objects and momentary graspings of eternal truths. There is no more reason to deny mortal knowledge of immortal verity than to deny the possibility of a picture in fireworks of the Rock of Gibraltar.

The intellect is not just the ability to acquire concepts: since concepts are themselves abilities, the intellect is also the ability to exercise concepts in appropriate conditions. The mind not only harvests ideas from experience, it gathers them in: it is the storehouse of ideas. Varying the metaphor, the intellect, when it commences its activity, is an unwritten tablet, a *tabula rasa*. As concepts and beliefs are acquired by the operation of the specifically human intelligence, the tablet becomes covered with writing, the empty barn fills up. The mind, we might say, has contents as well as powers. To find out the contents of a person's mind at a given time, you must find out what she understands, what she knows, what she believes at that moment.

The ideas, that is to say the concepts and beliefs, of the intellect are exercised in the course of the life whose intellect is in question. Just as the senses are necessary but not sufficient for the acquisition of ideas, so too sense and fancy are necessary for the exercise of ideas. If there is to be an exercise of concepts, or the application of knowledge, there must be some exercise of sense or fancy, some application to a sensory context. This seems to be true whether the concepts are concrete or abstract, whether the truths known are necessary or contingent.

For a man to be exercising the concept, say, of red, it seems that he must be either discriminating red from other colours around him, or having a mental image of redness, or a mental echo of the word 'red', or be talking, reading, or writing about redness, or something of the kind. He may indeed be able to *possess* the concept *red* without this showing in his experience of behaviour on a given occasion, but it seems that without some embodiment in sensory activity there could be no *exercise* of the concept on that occasion.

The case is the same with the knowledge of a general truth, such as that two things that are equal to a third are equal to each other. For this knowledge to be exercised it seems that its possessor must either enunciate it, or apply it say in the measurement of objects, or utilize it in some other way even if only in the artful manipulation of symbols.

10

Psychology

IN this final chapter I wish to discuss the scientific study of the mind. Can philosophy say anything about this in advance of empirical enquiry? Can philosophy set any limits to the possibility of psychological investigation?

Many people believe that the human mind is amenable to scientific enquiry in very much the same way as the human body is. Some believe that science is fundamentally deterministic, and that in principle there could be a deterministic science of the operation of the mind side by side with a deterministic science of the body. Not only the operation, but the origin, of the mind, many people believe, is something which science will shortly be able to explain. The theory of evolution by natural selection can account for the capacities of our minds no less than for the structure of our bodies.

In this final chapter I wish to investigate the credentials of these various forms of scientific optimism. Let us begin with a consideration of determinism.

Determinism is often defined as the view that every event has a cause. Neither *event* nor *cause* is as simple a notion as it looks. It is perfectly possible that if the two notions are given a clear and adequate analysis it may turn out that no consistent statement of determinism can be enunciated. But if we are to give a fair hearing to the claims of determinists, we should not assume such a conclusion in advance.

It is not easy to give a definition of 'event' which enables one to decide, for instance, how many events take place in a given region during a given period of time. The difficulty of giving such a definition places one obstacle in the way of a coherent formulation of determinism. For present purposes, however, I shall assume, without prejudice, that such difficulties can be overcome, and that among 'events', however the term is defined, will be included the movements of human bodies and the passing of thoughts through human minds.

In the subsequent discussion, by 'cause' I shall mean a particular kind of sufficient antecedent condition. The cause of an event, for purposes of this discussion, is a state or event preceding in time the event to be explained, such that it is a sufficient condition for the occurrence of such an event. This means that there is a covering law to the effect that whenever such a causal condition obtains, it is followed by an event of the appropriate kind. So if determinism is true, it will be the case for any event E that there was an antecedent event or state C such that there is a covering law to the effect that whenever a situation such as C obtains there will follow an event such as E. Every event will fall under a description such that there exists a law from which, in conjunction with a description of the antecedent conditions, it can be deduced that an event of that description will occur.

There are many types of determinism answering to this very rough and general scheme. The differences between types of determinism depend on the terms and concepts to be used in the description of the antecedent conditions and of the covering law. Indeed it is only the possibility of specifying types of description and types of law which prevents the scheme from being vacuous as a characterization of determinism. (No doubt one could formulate as a plausibly true covering law 'Whenever something happens, something else happens next'—but a determinism formulated in terms of this law would be of little interest.)

One form of determinism is couched simply in terms of logical laws. Since ancient times some philosophers have thought that it could be shown by pure logic that everything is determined by inexorable fate. 'What will be, will be' is undoubtedly a logical truth. From this truth many have sought to deduce the more interesting truth that what will be must be. They have tried to show, that is, that whatever happens could not have happened otherwise. This form of determinism is often called 'fatalism'. The purely logical arguments for fatalism are all fallacious, though it is often difficult, and may be highly instructive, to pin down exactly where they go astray.

Another form of determinism with a long history is theological determinism, which seeks to establish determinist conclusions not from pure logic, but from propositions of theology. According to theological determinism everything in the universe happens of necessity because the universe is the creature of an all-powerful and all-knowing God. Many have argued that if God knows everything from all eternity then everything must be determined from all eternity. Others have deduced determinism not from God's knowledge but from God's will and power. All the events of human history, many have believed, are not only foreknown but foreordained by God, so that even the most apparently free among human actions are the result of divine predestination.

More recently, other forms of determinism have been more in the forefront of academic discussion. The determinisms now most popular are determinisms in virtue of alleged economic or social or psychological or physiological laws. Fatalism and predestinarianism have been replaced by scientific determinism, determinism in virtue of the laws of some real or presumed science.

Many people believe that human actions are determined by the social or economic or familial environment of individuals. The claim is often made that someone with a complete knowledge of the histories of individuals and societies, and a complete mastery of the laws of the appropriate disciplines, would in principle be able to forecast their future. Among those who profess this kind of determinism many would claim some allegiance either to Marxism or Freudianism, though it is unclear how thoroughgoing and universal either Marx or Freud intended their own commitment to determinism to be. In their writings and those of their followers it is not always clear whether every detail of human history is supposed to be theoretically predictable, or whether even in principle the claim is only that the main lines of the development of individuals and society can be forecast.

Though there are many different kinds of determinism, deterministic theories can be grouped for philosophical purposes into two classes: psychological and non-psychological determinisms. By 'psychological determinisms' I mean determinisms whose characteristic laws contain mentalistic terms,

terms for mental events and states of mind. Non-psychological determinisms are those whose laws are statable without such terms. Henceforth I shall write as if there were just two types of determinism: psychological and non-psychological.

Psychological determinism has been popular among philosophers of certain schools for some centuries. In its traditional form psychological determinism regards action as determined by the wants and beliefs of agents. On this view, human behaviour is the outward resultant of internal motivating forces operating in the mind. Many contemporary kinds of determinism are psychological in the broad sense in which I am using the term. Freudian determinism is obviously psychological, since the entities of Freudian theory (such as the ego, the super-ego, and the id) and the forces invoked in Freudian explanation (such as the libido and the death-wish) are psychologically defined. But other forms of determinism too incorporate tacit mentalistic elements.

Economic determinism, for instance, is a form of psychological determinism to the extent that it uses mentalistic notions in the identification of its data and the formulation of its laws. Passing a dollar bill voluntarily over the counter is an economic phenomenon in a sense in which accidentally dropping a dollar bill down a drain is not: this is a distinction which can only be systematically applied in virtue of the relevant notion of *voluntariness*, which is a psychological concept. Notions such as purchase, property, and the profit motive all have explicit or tacit mentalistic components. Any determinism in virtue of economic laws will, therefore, be a psychological determinism.

It is characteristic of psychological determinism to treat the reasons and motives of actions as if they were the causes of those actions—causes which can be brought under the covering laws constitutive of the structure of determinism. In fact, reasons are not causes, and the relationship between reason and action is quite different from that between cause and effect.

Psychological determinism rests on the view that when we say that someone did something because he wanted to, the 'because' indicates a causal relationship. According to the psychological determinist, wants and beliefs are mental states or processes which stand in causal connection with bodily movements. For this to be the case, the mental events must be capable of separate identification from the physical events: they must be, as it were, separate items in the agent's biography. Moreover, these two kinds of events must be related by a causal law. But neither of these two conditions holds.

In the first place, mental events of the appropriate kind to figure in the causal relationship often simply do not take place. It is indeed true that every voluntary action must be an action that is in some sense wanted by the agent: if it were in no way wanted—not even, at the very minimum, reluctantly consented to—then it would not be voluntary. But an action may be voluntary without there being any mental event of wanting or choosing, distinguishable from the action itself, which precedes it or accompanies it. The choice of words when writing a letter is a voluntary act; sometimes there takes place, in imagination, a mental trying out of various forms of words, but very often there is nothing of the kind. In ordinary everyday conversation it would be absurd to say that each word uttered is preceded by a momentary mental episode which is the choice of the word. In the untypical cases where we do mentally rehearse the words we utter just before we speak them, this rehearsal is in its turn a voluntary action; but the rehearsal is not itself preceded by a rehearsal of the rehearsal.

Wants may occur, and an action may be correctly explained by reference to the want, without there being any mental event distinguishable from the action itself which manifests the want. The action and the explanatory want, therefore, are not the separately identifiable items of the agent's biography which they must be if the relation between them is to be a causal one.

Nor is the explanatory relation between a want and an action to be given in terms of a covering law. Wants do explain action, but they do so by the contribution which they make to the agent's reasons for acting. The psychological determinist thinks of reasons for action as being causes of action; but there is an important difference between reasons and causes. The rules which govern practical reasoning are of a totally different form from those which govern the operation of physical causes.

One important difference between the explanatory power of reasons and the operation of causes is this. If there is present a perfectly adequate cause for an effect, then the effect cannot but follow: for a cause—at least on the determinist's view of the matter—is a sufficient antecedent condition for the effect, and if an effect does not follow when an alleged cause is present we know the cause is not a genuine one. On the other hand there may be a perfectly adequate reason for performing an action and yet the action not ensue, without this fact casting any doubt on the adequacy of the reason.

Reasons explain actions that have actually been performed in the same way as practical reasoning leads to decisions about actions that are to be performed. Practical reasoning—reasoning about what to do—differs from theoretical deduction in an important way. As has been said earlier, practical reasoning is *defeasible*. That is to say, a conclusion which may be a reasonable one from a given set of premises may cease to be a reasonable one when further premises are added. (This is because the premisses of practical reasoning set out the goals to be achieved and the possibilities of achieving them: a decision which is reasonable in the light of a narrow set of goals may be inadequate in the light of a larger set.) Because rules of practical inference are defeasible, whereas causal laws are not, reasons cannot be regarded as causes.

All psychological forms of determinism are incoherent because they misconstrue the nature of the mental phenomena to which they explicitly or tacitly appeal in their formulation. Typically, psychological determinists think of wants as being mental events which determine action. But to say that someone did an act because he wanted to is not to postulate a mental event as causing an action through some spiritual mechanism whose operation is as yet imperfectly understood. A feeling of want is, of course, a mental event; but the wanting which makes the difference between voluntariness and non-voluntariness is not as such a mental event. I have typed the previous sentence voluntarily, and I chose each word of it; but there was no event of desiring or choosing the word, no act of wanting distinguishable from the inputting of the word itself. The cause–effect pattern which must be universal if determinism is to be true is not, in the case of psychological determinism, there to be generalized.

But the refutation of psychological determinism does not put paid to determinism, because not all forms of determinism are psychological. Physiological determinism, for instance, understood as the view that all human activity is determined via neurophysiological states of the brain and central nervous system, does not suffer from the internal incoherence which afflicts psychological determinism. The crucial question concerning physiological determinism is not so much the internal coherence of the theory as its relationship to our experience of human freedom. If the environment in which humans live is deterministic, and the human body is merely a complicated machine, can there be any genuinely free action?

We can only hope to answer this question if we have a firm grasp of what it means to describe action as free. Just as there are many versions of determinism, so there are many concepts of freedom. Like the versions of determinism, the concepts of freedom can for philosophical purposes be divided into two main classes. Some analyses of freedom lay most emphasis on the notion of choice or desire, others lay most emphasis on the notion of ability or power. Some define free will as the capacity to do what one wants, others define it as the power of action in the face of alternatives. On the one account, a person does something freely if he does it *because he wants to*; on the other account he does something freely if he does it *though it is in his power not to do it*. There are convenient, if archaic names for the two kinds of freedom: terms invented by the medieval scholastics, but surviving into later philosophers such as Hume. Freedom conceived in terms of choice or wanting is liberty of spontaneity; freedom conceived in terms of power to do otherwise is liberty of indifference.

When we ask whether determinism is compatible with freedom, it seems to make a difference which concept of freedom we take as our starting-point. Those who have argued for the compatibility of freedom and determinism have commonly favoured the conception of freedom as liberty of spontaneity and have often attacked the idea of liberty of indifference as incoherent and mythical. Many of these 'compatibilists'—as we may call them—have argued that there is no clash at all between the theory that all our acts are determined, and the experience that some of our actions are the results of our choices. We are free to act as we choose—so said these compatibilists—but our actions are determined because our choices in their turn are determined. We enjoy liberty of spontaneity, but not liberty of indifference; because if everything is determined then surely we never really have the power to do otherwise than we do.

Compatibilism of this kind is, in my view, mistaken. The issue of determinism and freedom cannot be simply resolved in this way by making a distinction between liberty of spontaneity and liberty of indifference. Each of the concepts of freedom is inseparably linked with the other. The two of them, as was argued earlier in Chapter 3, are two aspects of the single power of liberty.

The type of power to do otherwise which is necessary for freedom is the power to do otherwise if one wants to. As determinists have rightly insisted against libertarians, mere indeterminacy or randomness, such as that of elementary particles in quantum jumps, does not amount to anything like free will. So liberty of indifference, rightly understood, involves liberty of spontaneity. On the other hand it cannot be true that one acted because one wanted to unless one had in some measure and at some point the ability to act otherwise than one did. Liberty of spontaneity is impossible for someone who does not enjoy liberty of indifference. Liberty of spontaneity and liberty of indifference are two sides of the same coin.

The compatibilist who is also a psychological determinist is likely to deny that explanation of actions in terms of wants implies any alternative possibility of action. For an action to be free, he will say, it is enough for it to be done because it was wanted; and for it to be done because it was wanted, it is enough that it should have been caused by the want. There is no need for there ever to have been any real possibility that the action or the want should have been other than it in fact turned out to be. But this claim, we have already argued, is based on a mistaken assimilation of reasons to causes.

In the debate between libertarians and determinists, the libertarians have been right to insist against the determinists that there can be no genuine liberty in the absence of the power to do otherwise. The psychological determinist denies this only because he has inadequately analysed the concept of wanting. But it is not so clear that the libertarian is right to think that every form of determinism must rule out the power to do otherwise. It may be that the libertarian thinks this only because he has inadequately analysed the concept of power.

Freedom undoubtedly involves the power to do otherwise. I do X freely only if I have the power not to do X, and that means that I have the opportunity not to do X and the ability not to do X. Can this power ever be present if, say, physiological determinism is true? Can I have the ability and opportunity not to do X if I am in a physiological state from which, in conjunction with physiological laws, it can be deduced that my body will move in such a way that I will do X?

The answer, it seems to me, is that I can.

Consider first ability. Whether or not I have a given ability is settled by whether I fulfil the criteria for possessing that ability: that is to say, by whether I succeed in exercising it when there is an opportunity for exercising it and when I want to exercise it. Because abilities are inherently general, in order for me to fulfil these criteria on a particular occasion there is no need for me actually to exercise the ability on that occasion. And provided these criteria are fulfilled, it matters not what my current physiological state may be.

What of opportunity? Clearly, I may often have an opportunity, for example, to strangle my kitten even though I may not, on that occasion or on any other occasion, take advantage of that opportunity. But if I am in a physical position to strangle my kitten, but my current physiological state is such that I will not strangle him, can I really be said to have an opportunity to strangle him? Yes, indeed: there is nothing external to me preventing me. But, it might be argued, though there is nothing external to my body preventing me, is there not something external to my will preventing me, namely, the state of my brain and of my central nervous system? And if that is the case, surely the truth of physiological determinism would rule out the opportunity, and therefore the power, to strangle the kitten, and in general to act otherwise than I do.

The objection does not succeed, and it is important to see why. Physiological determinism need in no way involve the theory that wants do not affect actions: if it did, it could be dismissed out of hand as entailing an obvious falsehood. Any plausible physiological determinism must make room for such facts as that if I wanted to strangle the kitten I would. It follows that whatever story the physiological determinist tells about my present state must contain a proviso that my brain state would be different from what it now is if I wanted something different from what I now want (if, for instance, I wanted to strangle the kitten). Consequently, whatever my present state is, it is not a state such that if I wanted to strangle the kitten I could not. But only such a state would prevent me from strangling the kitten, or deprive me of an opportunity to strangle the kitten.

Physiological determinism, then, seems to leave room for both the ability and the opportunity to do otherwise than we do, and thus to be compatible with freedom, understood as liberty of indifference. But if—as this type of physiological determinism demands—every difference between wants is accompanied by a difference in physiological state, will not physiological determinism collapse into psychological determinism, which we have already rejected? No: physiological determinism would entail psychological determinism only if physiological events of a particular kind were correlated in a regular and law-like manner with psychological conditions of a particular kind. But there is no reason to believe that physiological determinism must involve such regular correlations.

It may be, for all we know, that for each individual case in which a human being can choose whether to do X or not to do X there is *a* difference between the state of the brain and of the central nervous system which goes with wanting to do X, and the state which goes with not wanting to do X; and this could well be the case without there being any general laws linking physiological states of a particular kind with psychological states of a particular kind. If this is so, there is no reason why physiological determinism should lead to psychological determinism, or why predictability at a physiological level should involve predictability at a psychological level.

I have been defending the theory that the freedom of the will is compatible with one kind of determinism. This theory, as I have observed, is sometimes called 'compatibilism': it is contrasted with the incompatibilism which regards freedom and determinism as irreconcilable. Sometimes compatibilism is identified with a philosophical theory which has been nicknamed 'soft determinism': but in reality the two positions are distinct. Soft determinism is a version of determinism: the soft determinist does believe that every event has a cause, in the sense of a sufficient antecedent condition. He is called 'soft' because he believes in addition that determinism does not exclude freedom: he is contrasted with the hard determinist who thinks that determinism is incompatible with freedom and that since determinism is true freedom must be an illusion. All soft determinists are incompatibilists but the converse is not true.

Though I have defended compatibilism, I am agnostic on the issue of determinism. I know of no convincing reason for believing universal determinism to be true, and no convincing reason for believing it to be false. I do not even know whether it can be given a totally coherent formulation. Most people who have a firm belief in determinism or indeterminism seem to me to base their conviction on an act of faith, or at best on an extrapolation from the history of science. But extrapolation from the history of science may incline one to determinism or to indeterminism in accordance with the particular science or the particular period of history from which one decides to extrapolate.

No doubt the commonest reason for believing in indeterminism is belief in incompatibilism. Since we know we are free agents, anyone who believes that freedom is incompatible with determinism is bound to conclude to indeterminism. But if compatibilism is defensible, there is no inference from freedom to indeterminism. The issue of compatibilism is a strictly philosophical issue: it is a question about the logical relationship between two sets of concepts. But on the assumption that determinism can be coherently formulated, the issue between determinists and indeterminists is not a purely philosophical question. The question concerns the nature of the system of laws governing the universe. If this question can be answered it cannot be answered by the philosopher alone. It is an issue on which the philosopher as such can and should remain agnostic.

The freedom which I have claimed to be compatible with determinism is the power of liberty which we defined in an earlier chapter. It is something which is not peculiar to human beings but applies to animals also. Is there anything in the nature of specifically human volition which excludes either determinism or indeterminism?

Some have argued that if physical science is ultimately deterministic, then mental science must also be, because states of mind are, in the last analysis, identical with physical states and if the physical states are determined the mental ones must be too. And I have earlier agreed that there is nothing incoherent in the idea that wherever human beings have the possibility of taking two alternative courses there is a physical difference between the physical state which would go with opting for one course and the physical state which would go with opting for the other.

Can we go further and identify states of mind with physical states? It is sometimes said that mental states and structures are simply physical states and structures described at a certain level of abstraction. But this is a misleading way of putting the truth: it suggests that one can identify an individual state, or an individual structure, as the individual entity it is, quite independently of describing it in mentalistic or physicalistic terms. But what counts as *the same individual* depends on what *kind* of individual is being described. The criteria of identity for a mental state are not the same as those for a physical state. Two people can be in the same physical state while being in a different mental state. Two people can be in the same mental state while being in a different physical state, and one person can continue in the same mental state while his physical state changes. In making this point against the materialist, one is not making any claim that a human being is an immaterial spirit. The same point can be made about computers: there is no one–one correlation between software structures and hardware structures.

The materialist is right in claiming that to describe a state of mind is to describe, at a certain degree of abstraction, a physical object. But the physical object which is described by mentalistic predicates is a human being, not a human brain. The brain states characteristic of speakers of English—if we assume, with the materialist, that there are such—may, for all we know, be reproducible *in vitro*. However successfully they were reproduced they would not constitute knowledge of English; for it is people, not brains, to whom it makes sense to attribute such knowledge.

Once again, this is not an argument for immaterialism. The same points can be made about pocket calculators no less than about human beings. My calculator works out the square root of 123456789. In a flash, there comes the answer 1111.11106. Between my pressing the square-root key and the display appearing, complicated events took place in its electronic innards. Those events, whatever they were, could have taken place in a different calculator doing a different job; and a different calculator doing the same job might well have taken an electronically totally different route. Moreover, the hardware might have been taken out of the case, separated from the input keys and the output display. Whatever electronic events then took place inside it would not have been the working-out of the square root of 123456789. For in the sense in which calculators can work out square roots for us, it is only whole calculators, and not portions of their electronic anatomy, however sophisticated, that can do the working-out.

Problems are caused by the use of the language of communication engineering in biology and in connection with computers and artificial intelligence. We have all become accustomed to talk of the genetic *code*, whereby sequences of four bases in the double helix of DNA determine the assembly of amino acids to make the proteins characteristic of particular organisms. The reason for calling it a code is that there is no known law specifying which group of bases in a strand of DNA determines which string of amino acids. The correlation seems quite arbitrary. But that is not enough to make it a code in the sense of a *language*: for that to be so the operation of the DNA would have to be by means of rules (like a chain of command) and not by causal mechanisms (like that of a template).

To see the difference think of a piano and a pianola. The holes in the pianola roll are correlated with the notes the pianola plays just as the notes on the page of the score are correlated with the notes the concert pianist plays. But the holes in the roll produce the notes causally; the note in the score guide the pianist's playing by rule. The holes in the roll are not symbols as the notes on the page are.

In general the fact that X is isomorphic to, and merely arbitrarily connected with, Y does not suffice to make X mean Y or be a symbol for Y. In addition it is necessary that X should be linked with Y by convention, and for that to be the case we need the intervention of voluntary agents acting intentionally according to rule.

If this were not so, the world would be full of symbols. Given suitable conventions, the fact that my car is parked outside my gate might express the fact that the Queen is in residence in Buckingham Palace. That is, if the car stands for the Queen, and the gate stands for the Palace, and the relation of being outside of stands for the relation of being inside of, we might conceive the car outside the gate as a sentence (false, as I write this) saying that the Queen is in residence in the Palace. The situation has the right logical multiplicity to represent, and the connection between the two situations is entirely arbitrary. But of course that is not enough. The car parked outside the gate is not a sentence, and that is because we have not set up the appropriate conventions; we do not use it as a symbol—though, of course, we might, if I was a modern gunpowder plotter wishing to have a system of signals for communication with a fellow-conspirator.

For something to be a linguistic representation of a state of affairs it not only needs to have the appropriate abstract structure, it needs to consist of elements conventionally correlated with elements of the structure to be represented. And conventions can only be set up by those who can *use* symbols: in the normal case, by human beings with the parts and passions of human beings. It is for this reason that we must deny that the elements in a computer bearing particular information *mean* that information, or, are symbols for that information. The output of a computer is meaningful and symbolic only to the extent that it is in a natural language or to the extent that appropriate conventions have been set up by the designers, programmers, and users of the computer.

If my brain were as deterministic as an electronic computer, so that its entire output could be predicted from the inputs it receives, that would not suffice for anyone to be able to predict the thoughts that I will have. For what gives meaning to any kind of output of my brain—whether channelled through action, speech, or writing—is something which is quite external to it, just as what gives meaning to the output of a computer is external to it. What gives meaning to my physical activities, what makes some of the sounds and gestures I produce into symbols, is my power to be a participant in the social activity of language—an activity which is impossible outside the context of the co-operation of others.

This point must be borne in mind also when we evaluate the suggestion that the human mind, like the human body, is the product of evolution. If this is to be true, then human language, just like the human brain and upright posture, must be something which has been produced by the processes of natural selection.

There are difficulties in principle in seeing how language could evolve by natural selection: language as we know it has features which are prima facie inexplicable by natural selection. Language, as we have just emphasized, is a social, conventional, rule-governed activity. Any account of how language evolved from other animal communication systems must take account of the fact that language involves the use of symbols. Symbols differ from other signs (traces, clues, symptoms) in being conventional and not natural signs.

When we say that language is conventional we do not mean that it was set up by some primeval linguistic social contract. Such a suggestion would be self-contradictory: obviously one cannot make a contract that a certain word is to mean X unless one already has the linguistic means of referring to X. Rather, we mean that the behaviour of language users is rule-governed. This means, among other things, that language-behaviour is not as such governed by causal regularities. One can keep a rule only if one can also break it. There is no law of nature to the effect that our utterances have the meaning they have.

There are several differences between rules governing behaviour and natural laws governing phenomena. One is that it is possible, and it often happens, that rules are violated. Short of a miracle it isn't possible for a natural law to be violated. If you find an apparent violation of a natural law you have an indication that the law has been wrongly stated. The occurrence of a violation of a rule, on the contrary, is no evidence that the rule has been wrongly framed.

Another difference is that if someone's behaviour is governed by rule he must be to some degree conscious of the rule. This does not mean that he must be able to formulate or enunciate the rule. It is notoriously hard for even a fluent language-speaker to enunciate the phonological, syntactic, and semantic rules he uses. What it means is that the user of a rule must be able to distinguish between correct and incorrect applications of the rule. He must know the difference between following and violating the rule if he can be said to be using the rule at all.

In contrast, one can be operated upon by a natural law without having any consciousness of it at all. For it to be true that mammals are procreated as a consequence of sexual congress there is no need for mammals to have any knowledge of this fact. On the other hand if a linguistic community operates a certain rule for transforming indicative sentences into interrogative ones the members of the community must be capable of distinguishing between well-formed and ill-formed interrogatives.

Now the rule-governed nature of languages makes it difficult to explain the origin of language by natural selection. The explanation by natural selection of the origin of a feature in a population presupposes the occurrence of that feature in particular individuals of the population. Horses, for instance, may have developed the length of their legs through evolutionary stages. One can very easily understand how natural selection might favour a certain length of leg: if it were advantageous to have long legs, then the long legged individuals in the population might outbreed the others. Clearly, where such explanation of the occurrence of features is most obviously apposite, it is perfectly possible to conceive the occurrence of the feature in single individuals. There is no problem about describing a single individual as having legs n metres long. (There may or may not be a problem about explaining the origin of the single long-legged specimen; but there is no logical difficulty in the very idea of such a favoured specimen.)

Now it does not seem at all plausible to suggest, in a precisely parallel way, that the human race may have begun to use language because the language-using individuals among the population were advantaged and so outbred the non-language-using individuals. This is not because it is difficult to see how spontaneous mutation could produce a language-using individual; it is because it is difficult to see how anyone could be a language-user at all before there was a community of language-users.

In writing this book I am using language, and that I am doing so depends no doubt on decisions of my own and is conditioned in all kinds of ways by the physiology of my own body. But whatever I did, whatever marks I made on paper or keys I tapped on a keyboard, they could not have the meaning my words now have were it not for the existence of conventions not of my making, and the activities of countless other users of English.

If we reflect on the social and conventional nature of language, we see something odd in the idea that language may have evolved because of the advantages possessed by language-users over non-language-users. It seems almost as odd as the idea that golf may have evolved because golf-players had an advantage over non-golf-players in the struggle for life, or that banks evolved because those born with a cheque-writing ability were better off than those born without it.

Of course, in fact, games like golf and institutions like banks were not evolved by natural selection: they were invented or developed through the voluntary choices of human beings. One could not explain the origin of language in the same way. In order to be able to invent an instrument for a particular purpose you need to be able to conceive the purpose in advance and devise the invention as a means of achieving the purpose. It is not possible that someone who did not have a language could first of all conceive a purpose that language could serve and then devise language as a means to serve it. Nor could language be hit upon by accident, as some human procedures were—as in the legend that pork was first roasted when somebody's house was burnt down with his pig inside. One cannot conceive of somebody's being the first person accidentally to follow a set of linguistic rules, as one can conceive of him being the first accidentally to set fire to his house.

The difficulty, then, is that an individual's behaviour is not linguistic behaviour except in the context of the behaviour of others. But is not this true of all kinds of social behaviour, including some of which dumb animals are undoubtedly capable? A courtship ritual would not be what it is without the responsive behaviour of the mate. Nor, for that matter, would sexual organs be sexual organs if it were not for the corresponding organs of the opposite sex. So there seems no more difficulty in accounting for the evolution of language than in accounting for the evolution of sexual organs or courtship rituals.

Both parallels break down. Sexual anatomy can be described, just as long legs can, without reference to the counterpart anatomy, though of course its function in procreation cannot be brought out without reference to the counterpart. But the difficulty concerns utility, not conceivability. The cases given are not parallel to the sharing of rules between language-users. The linguistic parallel to them would be facts such as that for species-specific communication the sounds used to communicate must be audible to other members of the same species.

The parallel between language and ritualized animal activity also breaks down, though ritual activities do occupy an intermediate position between causally efficacious activity and genuine language. Ritual activities resemble language in not being part of a mechanism operated to produce an effect causally. They differ from language in that their essence consists in specifiable behaviour rather than in a set of rules of representation.

Linguistic activity cannot be given a precise behavioural specification, because many different behaviours may be the same linguistic act. For instance, I use the expression 'No Smoking' whether I say it or write it, but the behaviour involved in writing it is totally different from that involved in saying it. This does not mean that it is the invention of writing rather than the origin of speech that marks the boundary between human language and animal communication. It means rather that the way in which human language is conventionalized is quite different from the way in which animal behaviours are ritualized. For part of what we mean when we say that human language is conventional is that *any kind of behaviour* will do provided that it obeys the right rules. Not only speaking and writing but morse code, semaphore, American sign-language, etc. can be used to utter the very same sentence, given the appropriate conventions. Indeed, it underestimates the crucial function of rules in language to say that language is *governed* by rules. Language is rather *constituted* by rules. Take any human sign-language: you can change anything in the sign apart from the rules governing the use and the language will remain the same. Courtship rituals provide no parallel to this.

Animal systems of communication can, of course, be very efficient in communicating information to one animal about another. But the kind of communication involved is not the kind of communication characteristic of language. Human beings communicate information to each other in many ways other than by the use of articulate language: by gesture, by expression, by tone of voice, by body language in general. If you overhear a conversation in a neighbouring railway compartment you can often get a lot of information about the age, the sex, the temper, of those involved. You may come to realize, for example, that there is an old woman who is very angry with a small child who is being naughty. But you can acquire this information without hearing any of the actual words said, or without understanding any of them if they are uttered in a language one does not understand. It is this, not the understanding of language, which is the human analogue to the communication of information by animals.

The difficulty then in using the principles of selection to explain the origin of language is a unique one, differing from the problems in explaining other phenomena. The difficulty may not be insuperable, but it is rare to find it seriously faced.

Bibliographical Note

My greatest debt throughout this book is to the works of Wittgenstein, especially *Philosophical Investigations* (Blackwell, Oxford, 1953). I have tried to present a popular account of Wittgenstein's thought in *Wittgenstein* (Penguin, Harmondsworth, 1973) and I have related Wittgenstein's work to that of other philosophers and psychologists in the papers reprinted in *The Legacy of Wittgenstein* (Blackwell, Oxford, 1984). The two books which most helped me to understand and to see the importance of Wittgenstein's philosophy of mind were G. E. M Anscombe's *Intention* (Blackwell, Oxford, 1957) and P. T. Geach's *Mental Acts* (Routledge, London, 1958).

Chapter 1. The views attributed to Descartes are critically elucidated, with original passages cited in justification, in my book *Descartes* (Random House, New York, 1968). The anti-Cartesian arguments here and elsewhere derive from Wittgenstein's argument against private languages, as expounded in my *Wittgenstein*, chapter 10, and in my paper 'Cartesian Privacy' (*The Anatomy of the Soul*, Blackwell, Oxford, 1973, pp. 113–28). The neo-Cartesianism of recent years is illustrated by N. Chomsky, *Rules and Representations* (Blackwell, Oxford, 1980) and Paul M. Churchland, *Matter and Consciousness* (MIT Press, Cambridge, 1984); see my 'Language and the Mind' in *The Legacy of Wittgenstein*, chapter 10.

Chapter 2. The account of mind given here is a development of that presented in *Will, Freedom and Power* (Blackwell, Oxford, 1975), chapter 1, and in the Edinburgh Gifford lectures of 1971–2 and 1972–3, *The Nature of Mind* and *The Development of Mind* (Edinburgh University Press, 1972 and 1973). Some of its most recent developments were presented in the Glasgow Gifford lectures of 1988, forthcoming. The view with which it most starkly contrasts is presented in S. C. Stich, *From Folk Psychology to Cognitive Science*, (MIT Press, Cambridge, 1983).

Chapter 3. The account of the will given here is a development of that presented in *Action, Emotion and Will* (Routledge, London, 1963), chapters 10–11, and *Will, Freedom and Power*, chapters 2–4. Applications in legal contexts have been studied in *Freewill and Responsibility* (Routledge, London, 1978) and in *The Ivory Tower*, (Blackwell, Oxford, 1985).

Chapter 4. This chapter is based on chapters 1–5 of my *Action, Emotion and Will,* revised in the light of criticisms of that book, in particular that of Justin Gosling in 'Emotion and Object', *Philosophical Review,* 74 (1965), 486–503. My original chapters were heavily indebted to then unpublished writings of Wittgenstein which were later published in *Zettel* (Blackwell, Oxford, 1964).

Chapter 5. The account of ability presented here has been developed in a number of places: *Will, Freedom and Power,* chapter 7; *Freewill and Responsibility,* chapter 2. The account of the distinction between intellect and will was first presented in a paper, 'Descartes on the Will', in *The Anatomy of the Soul* and has undergone substantial modification in a number of papers since then. The analysis of the notion of 'disposition' was first undertaken in the apparatus to my edition of articles 49–54 of the Ia IIae of St Thomas Aquinas in volume 22 of the Blackfriars edition of the *Summa Theologiae* (Eyre and Spottiswoode, London, 1964). For a different way of understanding the notion of faculty, see J. A. Fodor, *The Modularity of Mind,* (MIT Press, Cambridge, 1983).

Chapter 6. This chapter is an abbreviation and development of my Aquinas lecture *The Self,* published by Notre Dame University Press (South Bend) in 1988. The contemporary view of the self there controverted is taken especially from T. Nagel, *The View from Nowhere* (OUP, Oxford, 1986).

Chapter 7. The Aristotelian theory of sensation, here defended in a modified form, is discussed, with original passages in justification, in my papers 'The Argument from Illusion in Aristotle's Metaphysics' *Mind,* 76 (1967), 184–97 and 'Intentionality: Aquinas and Wittgenstein', in *The Legacy of Wittgenstein,* chapter 5. The theory of secondary qualities put forward by Descartes is expounded and criticized in the final chapter of my *Descartes.*

Chapter 8. My own analysis of the concept of imagination was developed in criticism of Aquinas' theory of the phantasm, as critically presented in a series of papers beginning with 'Intellect and Imagination in Aquinas', in *Aquinas,* a series of critical essays edited by A. Kenny (Doubleday, New York, 1968).

Chapter 9. My first attempt to develop a theory of intentionality, following the lead of Geach, is in *Action, Emotion and Will,* chapter 9. Among recent treatments from which I have learnt, I would single out John Searle's *Intentionality* (CUP, Cambridge, 1983).

Chapter 10. The particular version of compatibilism here defended has been presented in *Will, Freedom and Power,* chapters 7–8, and *Freewill and Responsibility,* chapter 2. The discussion of the evolution of language is a development of one of my 1973 Gifford lectures in *The Development of Mind*.

The earlier books and papers of mine referred to in this note contain full references to the authors from whom I have borrowed or whom I have controverted.

Index